The Referees' Quiz Book

ERRATA

Question 42 on page 25 refers to diagram on page 26.

Second line of answer 106 on page 79 should continue
"corner kick, throw-in or when the ball is dropped by the . . ."

The Referees' Quiz Book

Reg Paine

**An Official Publication of the
Football Association**

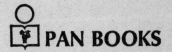 PAN BOOKS

First Published by Pan Books Ltd
18 Cavaye Place SW10 · 1976

© The Football Association 1976

ISBN 0 330 24847 2

Printed in Great Britain by
Richard Clay (The Chaucer Press) Ltd, Bungay, Suffolk

Contents

Introduction

It is said that there is nothing new under the sun and this applies to football in general and this book in particular. The author of the book is Reg Paine, who is the Referees' Secretary of the Football Association. He is an ex-Football League Referee, having retired a few seasons ago upon reaching the League's age-limit of forty-seven, and is also a qualified F.A. Coach. He has written this book from his knowledge of the Laws of the Game together with the information published from time to time in F.A. Memoranda and guidance given by other governing bodies.

I am sure that greater knowledge of the Laws of the Game would lead to a better understanding and appreciation of the spirit of the game, thereby assisting in reducing violence, misconduct and foul play in football; and one of the purposes of this book is to assist towards that end.

This book should not just be looked on as another quiz book for Referees, nor is it intended as a substitute for the *Referees' Chart and Players' Guide to the Laws of Association Football*. It is a book to which the aspiring Referee can refer to build up his knowledge of the game and thus improve his refereeing ability. It is hoped that it will prove of use to the more established Referee who will be able to refer to it for an authoritative answer on any particular problem – authoritative because facts mentioned and answers given to the questions will be based on the Laws of the Game or an official decision or statement. The average player and spectator will also be able to derive benefit from these pages and not only enjoy his football more but appreciate the problems that confront the referee.

It is anticipated that revised editions will become available from time to time as the Laws of the Game are amended.

E. A. CROKER
Secretary — The Football Association

Foreword

This book consists of a series of questions on the seventeen Laws of the Game and their practical application. It is a serious attempt to highlight the problems and difficulties that confront the Referee at all levels of the game. The book is divided into sections designed to keep together the various connected Laws.

The answers to the questions appear on pages 53 to 94 at the back of the book. The short articles and comments that appear are placed in the section appropriate to the applicable Law.

The Laws of the Game referred to are published in the *Referees' Chart and Players' Guide to the Laws of Association Football*, published by Pan Books at 40p.

Glossary

I.B.D. means International Board Decision. (Each Law except Law 17 has International Board Decisions and these are numbered for easy reference.)

F.I.F.A. Q & A means *Federation of International Football Associations' Questions and Answers*.
Advice to Referees appears after each Law except Law 2 in the *Referees' Chart*.

F.A. Guide for Referees and Linesmen is a Football Association publication, and can be purchased from the Football Association, 16 Lancaster Gate, London W2 3LW.

Know the Game, published for the Football Association by Educational Productions Limited, can also be obtained from the above address, as well as from booksellers.

The International Football Association Board

It must be emphasized that the Laws of the Game are kept as simple as possible and major amendments are rarely made. Even minor alterations are not approved before very considerable discussion and debate by the affiliated countries culminating in an annual meeting of the International Football Association Board.

The first International Conference was held in December 1882. Each of the four British National Football Associations was represented and the result of this important Conference was the establishment of the International Football Association Board, which body alone was given the power to alter or amend the Laws of the Game.

At the present time, of course, F.I.F.A. are also members of this Law-formulating Board, thus ensuring that the Laws of Association Football are recognized throughout the world and apply equally to all matches at senior and junior level. There are but seventeen Laws and they have evolved gradually as the outcome of more than a hundred years' experience. At the annual meeting of the Board the four British Associations have one vote each and F.I.F.A. have four votes, making a total of eight votes. For any amendment or addition to the Laws of the Game to be approved, six votes out of the total number of eight are required.

It is impossible to legislate for every circumstance that might arise during the playing of a football match. Outside the strict application of the Law, there may be incidents that can only be dealt with under the powers, guidance and common sense of the Referee. The character and spirit of the game depend to a very large extent upon the willing co-operation of the players in complying with the Laws and accepting the decisions of the Referee.

Questions

Whether you are a junior or a senior player, a junior or a senior Referee, a coach, a manager, a spectator or even an armchair enthusiast, it is hoped that from this book you will learn something of benefit which will enable you to enjoy a little more this great game of football.

Fouls and Misconduct

We will 'kick off' with an important and interesting subject, which is probably the most controversial and topical of all aspects of football and which creates more problems than it should. I refer to MISCONDUCT AND FOUL PLAY.

1 For what reasons may a player be sent from the field of play?

2 Under what headings may a Referee officially caution a player?

3 An attacker attempts to kick the ball whilst it is securely held by the goalkeeper. What action should be taken by the Referee?

4 It is a common practice nowadays for goalkeepers when attempting to catch a high ball to raise a foot or knee at an angle, i.e. an outstretched position, as they jump for the ball. Is this an infringement of the Laws?

5 There are nine offences that are punishable by the award of a penalty-kick if they are committed by a player in his own penalty area. What are these offences?

6 There are technical infringements for which the Referee should award an indirect free-kick, e.g. playing the ball twice at a free-kick, throw-in, kick-off at the start of a match, etc. If a player is officially cautioned for dissent without any other breach of the Law having occurred, an indirect free-kick would also be awarded. Off-side is similarly punished. There are other offences perhaps more involved with the actual playing of the game for which the punishment is an indirect free-kick. Name as many of these offences as you can.

7 If a defending player is ordered off the field for kicking an opponent whilst within his own penalty-area, should a penalty-kick be awarded?

8 If the ball is about to be dropped by the Referee within the penalty-area and the defending player strikes an opponent before the ball touches the ground, what action should the Referee take?

9 If a player enters the field of play without the permission of the Referee and then commits a more serious infringement, how should he be penalized?

10 What should a Referee do when a player, having already been cautioned, commits a second cautionable offence?

11 If during a game a Referee cautions a player and at the conclusion of the match the player sincerely apologizes, should the Referee omit to report the caution?

12 If a player intentionally pulls an opponent's shirt, what is the punishment?

13 What action should the Referee take if two players of the same team exchange several blows?

14 If you are the Referee what would be your decision if a goal-keeper threw the ball violently and deliberately into the face of an opponent?

15 If a defender interposes his body between his goalkeeper in possession of the ball and an attacker who is attempting to charge the goalkeeper, what action should the Referee take?

16 If a player deliberately turns his back to an opponent when he is about to be tackled, may he be charged?

17 If an attacking player makes physical bodily contact with the goalkeeper in his goal area when the goalkeeper is not in possession of the ball but they are both attempting to play the ball, is this an infringement?

18 May a player 'climb up' on the shoulders of a colleague in order to attempt to head the ball?

19 What action is taken if a player spits at an opponent?

20 A goalkeeper standing outside his penalty-area reaches out and handles the ball inside the penalty-area. Has an infringement of the laws occurred?

21 What action should the Referee take if a defending player other than the goalkeeper intentionally handles the ball inside the penalty-area whilst he is standing outside the penalty-area?

22 What action should the Referee take if two players of the same team engage in violent conduct when they are both off the field of play but the ball is in play?

23 Is it an offence if a goalkeeper lies on the ball for an unnecessary length of time?

24 If a player unintentionally plays the ball with his hand and thereby gains an advantage, what action should the Referee take?

25 What action should the Referee take if a player shouts 'OK it's mine' as he and an opponent attempt to play the ball?

26 If a named substitute should enter the field of play without the Referee's permission and intentionally handle the ball in his own penalty area, thus preventing the ball from entering the goal, what action should the Referee take?

27 Why should dangerous play not be regarded as seriously as foul play; i.e. only an indirect free-kick be awarded for dangerous play whereas a direct free-kick is awarded for foul play?

28 Should the Referee stop the game for a player who is slightly injured?

29 If a player commits an act of misconduct during the half-time interval may the Referee take action?

30 If a defender fouls an opponent outside the penalty-area and both players are carried by their momentum into the penalty-area, should the Referee award a direct free-kick outside the area or a penalty?

31 Is a competition permitted to include a new rule in its regulations, giving authority for the introduction of the 'Sin Bin' system, whereby a player may be sent from the field for a specified period according to the seriousness of the infringement instead of being cautioned?

32 If an attacker and a defender in jumping for the ball but failing to make contact with it fall into the back of the net behind the goal-line, and the defender intentionally kicks the attacker while they are on the ground, should the Referee award a penalty?

33 If the captain of a team sees one of his players commit an act of serious misconduct, may he order him from the field?

34 A player requests permission to leave the field which the Referee grants, and as he is so doing the ball comes towards him and he shoots and scores. What action should the Referee take?

35 If, while the ball is in play, a player intentionally strikes an opponent who is in an off-side position and standing in the penalty-area but not interfering with play in any way, should a penalty be awarded?

36 If at the taking of a goal-kick a player outside the penalty area is deliberately tripped before the ball has passed out of the penalty-area, should a free-kick be awarded?

37 A throw-in has been awarded, and before it is taken an incident occurs in the penalty-area when a defender kicks an attacker. What action should the Referee take?

38 What would be the Referee's decision if just as the goalkeeper is running to play the ball within his own goal-area he is fairly charged by an opponent?

39 If, as the goalkeeper runs out to play a ball very close to the penalty-mark an attacker, who is running in, charges him fairly and gets possession, what action should the Referee take?

40 If a player is fouled but the Referee allows play to continue because there is a definite advantage to the offended team, may the Referee take disciplinary action later?

Technical Requirements

We have just dealt with a very important aspect of Association Football: physical contact, fair and unfair, and the problems that arise.

As well as factors concerning the actual playing of the game there are technical requirements necessary to the game, such as the playing area, the ball and the players' equipment. The average spectator does not need to know the laws covering these matters in great detail but the Referee needs to learn the requirements in order to pass his qualifying examination and in order to continue with his practical refereeing.

The skills of the game have undoubtedly been improved by the advances in technique made in the manufacture of footballs and players' equipment and in the preparation and maintenance of pitches. In June 1957 the International Board made the following statement:

'The constant striving for improvement in facilities and equipment is a clear sign of the healthy development of the game. Much of the progress in this direction stems from countries that have been ready to experiment with new ideas including flood-lighting, lightweight clothing and boots, screw-in studs, valve footballs, water-proofing and colouring footballs, luminous flags. Through the influence of the International Board and F.I.F.A. there is a growing recognition of the need to improve standards, and to define them in order to bring about more uniform conditions of play the world over.

Law 1 THE FIELD OF PLAY.

(a) The dimensions of the field of play were laid down within fairly wide limits in order to provide for all types of football, from junior to senior and international grades. The extension of the number of matches between teams of different nationalities points to the need for some degree of standardization of dimensions. It is recommended that all fields on which games between teams of different countries are played should, whenever possible, conform to the dimensions of 115 yards by 75 yards (103.82 metres by 69 metres)

(b) It is difficult to legislate for the conditions of the playing surface, but it is felt that high standards should be sought after, especially in terms of a level and even surface. Marking should be by liquid drying

(c) With the greater use of flood-lighting, it is recommended that a minimum standard of illumination should be 1500 kw, preferably from a height of more than 75 ft.'
(N.B. Standards of flood-lighting have, of course, been raised over the years, especially since the introduction of colour television.)

Great improvements have been made in connection with football-boot studs and it was in 1951 that for the first time studs were permitted that were shaped as truncated cones, provided that the diameter was not less than half an inch. At this time studs were only legal if they were made of leather or rubber.

In 1955 the law was again amended, so that studs could be constructed of leather, rubber, aluminium, plastic or similar material.

In 1965 a survey was carried out amongst the ninety-two Football League Clubs, and the over-all opinion was that plastic and nylon studs were no more dangerous than leather studs *provided* that proper attention was given to them in the normal course of wear. Each Club in the Football League was invited to give its comments, and only one Club commented on the fact that a serious injury had resulted from a dangerous nylon stud. Many Clubs were of the opinion that nylon studs tended to become serrated more quickly than other studs, especially if the player had to walk on concrete from the dressing-room to the field. In other words, it was felt that great attention should be paid to frequent checks on this type of stud.

The appropriate law now provides for the moulded stud to be smaller than the screw-in type stud, provided there is a minimum of ten to each shoe or boot.

The progress in the manufacture of footballs has had a tremendous bearing on the skills of the game. At one time the laws stipulated that 'the outer casing shall be of leather'. At the International Board Meeting prior to the commencement of the Season 1965-66, this wording was altered to read 'the outer casing shall be of leather or other approved materials', and Decision No. 2 was amended to read, 'The International Board from time to time shall decide what constitutes approved materials . . .' Since this time, many different types of balls not constructed of leather have been approved.

Because of the world shortage of leather and the technological progress by manufacturers, it was decided at the International Board Meeting held in June 1973 that

23

footballs would be approved on the basis of size, weight and pressure. It is, of course, permissible for any competition to stipulate the type of ball that shall be used in their matches, provided they conform to the Laws of the Game.

In the Football Association's Memorandum No. 6, issued in 1952, the regulations were detailed regarding light-coloured and water-proofed footballs.

It seems difficult to believe that at one time, when leather footballs were the only approved ball, a 16 oz ball, after forty-five minutes' play on a wet muddy day, weighed approximately 19 oz. Once the water-proofed ball was in use, and its qualities of retaining its liveliness and bounce were apparent, its popularity grew, and the all-important factor that it did not increase in weight made it the only type of ball that players wanted to use. Light-coloured balls of course became popular when weather conditions were inferior and the Football Association in 1952 decided that 'a referee had power at any point in the game to allow the substitution of a lighter coloured ball when by so doing he considered that his control of the match would be made easier'. It was accepted then and it is most apparent now that it is preferable for the same type of ball to be used throughout the entire match.

Law 1 quotes other technical details regarding the field of play and its appurtenances, such as shape of goal-posts and cross-bar and materials permitted in their construction.

The fitness of a pitch may at times present problems to a referee. He must decide whether a game can start or, having started, be continued, and has to take into account such conditions as snow, mud, water, ice and fog.

The safety of the players is always the most important factor to be considered by the referee in deciding whether or not a pitch is playable.

The condition of the pitch, especially in senior football,

which is a spectator sport, the possibility of 'reasonable' play and the ability of the players to exercise their skills must also be taken into account. Also in senior football the safety of the terraces where the spectators will stand must be given due consideration as must the visibility for the spectators, as well as for the Referee, his linesmen and the players.
In top league football the Referee has on occasions to make a decision several hours before the game in order to avoid unnecessary travel for supporters.

41 What are the requirements of the Law regarding the size of the playing field?

42 There are definite requirements regarding the measurement of the goal-area, penalty-area, centre circle, corner-quadrants, height of corner-posts, dimensions of goal-posts and cross-bar width between goal-posts, height from ground to the underside of the cross-bar and thickness of lines.

43 What is the distance (inside meaurement) between the goal-posts?

44 How far from the ground is the lower edge of the cross-bar?

45 Are goal-nets an essential requirement of the laws of the game?

46 May a pitch be marked out in creosote?

47 What is the maximum width of the lines?

48 If a penal offence is committed by a defender on the line of the penalty-area, is the punishment the award of a free-kick or a penalty-kick?

Complete the diagram measurements below:
What are the distances between the following points?

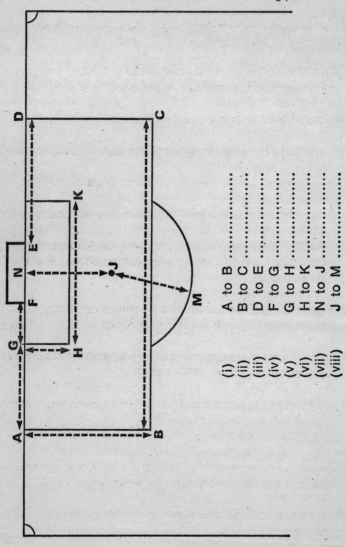

(i) A to B ....
(ii) B to C ....
(iii) D to E ....
(iv) F to G ....
(v) G to H ....
(vi) H to K ....
(vii) N to J ....
(viii) J to M ....

49 What is the minimum height of the corner flag-posts from the ground?

50 Are flag-posts opposite the half-way line on each side of the field of play essential?

51 If the cross-bar becomes displaced or broken may the game continue, with a rope being used as a substitute?

52 What should be the circumference of a football?

53 What should be the weight of a regulation-sized football?

54 Are there any restrictions on the colours of the ball?

55 If the ball is half-way over the touch line is it out of play?

56 If the ball bursts during the course of the game and whilst play is in progress, what action should the Referee take?

57 A team comprises not more than eleven players; is it essential that one of them is nominated as a goalkeeper?

58 What is the minimum number of players necessary per team before the start of the match?

59 How many substitutes are permitted for each team during
      (a) A competition match?
      (b) A friendly match?

60 May a player return to the field of play and take further part in the game if he has earlier been substituted?

61 May a substitution take place whilst the game is in progress?

62 May an injured player come back on to the field after receiving treatment whilst the game is in progress?

63 What action should the Referee take if a player enters the field without his permission?

64 May an out-field player change places with the goalkeeper and if so under what circumstances?

65 If the goalkeeper changes places with an out-field player without the Referee's permission and the 'new goalkeeper' then handles the ball, what offence is committed?

66 How must a substitution be carried out?

67 May a player be ordered off the field before the game commences?

68 A team starts short of three players – two of the missing players arrive during the first half, and the third, 10 minutes before the end of the second half.
May they be permitted to take part in the game?

69 What action would the Referee take if after 20 minutes' play he discovered that one of the teams had twelve players on the field?

70 If a player in possession of the ball passes over the touchline, keeping the ball in play in order to beat an opponent, should he be penalized for leaving the field without permission?

71 If a player with an injured arm protects his injury with a plaster bandage, what action should the Referee take?

72 May a player take part in a game wearing ordinary shoes instead of the customary football footwear?

73 Are nylon studs permissible in accordance with the Laws of the Game?

74 May a player wearing a track suit take part in a match?

75 Has a Referee the right to ask a player to remove a ring from his finger?

76 May a player take part in a competitive match wearing spectacles?

77 May a goalkeeper wear a black jersey if the Referee is also wearing a black uniform?

78 A substitute enters the field without the Referee's permission and strikes an opponent, who retaliates by striking him back. Both players must be dismissed from further participation in the game. Does this mean that one team will play with only ten men on the field whilst the other team (that of the player entering the field illegally) will continue to play with eleven men, since none of their players on the field were guilty of any offence?

79 Has a Referee jurisdiction over photographers adjacent to the field of play?

80 If a player is injured during the pre-match warm up before the game starts, may he be replaced by another player?

81 What is the prime factor regarding players' equipment with which the Referee has to be concerned?

The Officials

The responsibility and power accorded to the Referee in pursuance of the Laws the Game are not generally appreciated by the average football spectator or even the average player. It can be fairly stated that the extent of the responsibility of the Referee increases with the importance of the match in as much as there are increasing tensions and pressures on the players and the crowd. Every decision made in an important match is subject to closer scrutiny and criticism than in a more junior encounter.

The Referee needs to show qualities of man-management, authority and understanding of the players and their problems in order to maintain control, and these factors are important in all games. In senior football, where neutral Linesmen are appointed, it is important for the co-operation between the three officials to be of the highest order.

The questions in this section will be devoted to the duties of the Referee and his Linesmen, and the problems facing them. It will be generally accepted that Referees' decisions can frequently be unpopular, and in the following passage Don Revie, the England Team Manager, poses the question 'Who would be a Referee?'

WHO WOULD BE A REFEREE?

For a pittance each week they subject themselves to abuse and protest at the hands of players, managers, public and press. Their reward is the satisfaction derived from their task for which they train in their spare time to maintain fitness. They are never 'right' and very rarely have a 'good game'! With the escalation of rich rewards available to today's top footballing stars and Clubs, the Referee's job has gone from difficult to well-nigh impossible. On his decision may well rest the result of a match, whether to give a penalty or not, off-side or a goal. There must always be an aggrieved party in such an adjudication who can call to aid his 'prosecution' slow-motion replays and press photography. These after-match devices can be used to show the Referee was wrong in a decision given in a split second amidst the fast-moving action. When the incident is slowed down and re-run three times he may well be proved wrong; the point is surely obvious. The Referee has the most difficult job in football. He is both human and part-time and mistakes must occur. Indeed it is a credit to the Referees that so few do. Just as there are good players and bad players, so it is with Referees . . . The difficulty arises from non-participatory criticism – the spectator who makes his accusation from the comfort and perfect view of the stand, the television replay which takes away the very factor which makes mistakes inevitable – the speed of the action.

However the position is rationalized, the Referee will continue to be abused by the aggrieved, for football is a sport of emotion allied to rich rewards and fame. All credit to Referees and for their dedication and acceptance of an unenviable position. I certainly would not be one.

DON REVIE,
England Team Manager.

82 Name as many of the Referee's duties and powers as you can.

83 Must a Referee penalize all infringements of the Laws?

84 If the Referee terminates the game for any reason before its conclusion may he decide that either of the teams is disqualified and loses the match?

85 May a team manager or coach give instructions from the touch-line, (in a calm and orderly manner) whilst the game is in progress.

86 When in accordance with the Laws does the authority of the Referee commence?

87 If a player commits two offences at the same time, what action should the Referee take?

88 If the Referee awards a goal may he alter his decision?

89 If the Referee is struck by the ball which temporarily stuns him and the ball then enters the goal, should the score be allowed to stand, although the Referee did not see it?

90 Must the Referee take notice of information given by a neutral Linesman and act thereon regarding an incident that he (the Referee) has not seen?

91 If the Referee allows an advantage for a foul and it does not benefit the offended team, may he then award a free-kick or a penalty-kick as appropriate?

92 May the offending player in an advantage situation be dealt with for the offence even though the Referee has not stopped play or awarded a free-kick etc.?

93 The ball passes over the goal-line and the Linesman signals for a corner-kick but before the Referee has confirmed his decision a defender in his own penalty-area strikes an attacker. What offence has been committed and how should the Referee restart the match?

94 If the two captains agree to play on after the first half without any interval, may one of the players insist on his right to 5 minutes rest?

95 The Referee's decision is final but only if based on fact. Remembering this, has a League the right to ask a Referee why he allowed or did not allow a goal in a particular match?

96 What essential equipment does a Referee need to take on to the field?

97 In acordance with the existing regulations is it permissible for all senior Referees to officiate as a Referee at an international match?

98 What action may a Referee take regarding a Linesman who is inefficient, biased or unco-operative?

99 Whose responsibility is it to supply the Linesmen's flags?

100 A team is disatisfied with a Referee's decision and walks off the field. After several minutes in the dressing-room the team expresses a wish to restart the game. Should the Referee accede to this request?

101 Before the start of a match the Referee notices or is informed that one of the players is under suspension. May the Referee refuse to allow him to play in that game?

102 May a Referee allow a player who has been sent off in the first half to return after half-time if he apologizes for the incident?

103 Should a Referee take action against a player who lights a cigarette during the game?

Off-Side

The off-side law and its application probably causes more discussion amongst spectators than any other Law of the Game and it is important to remember certain official statements that have been made from time to time.
In September 1969 F.I.F.A. made this statement:

> *Off-side* If the ball is in play and has been last played by or has touched an opponent before it reaches a player in an off-side position, this player cannot be given off-side. This is laid down in the Law. Referees are advised that when the ball is played forward to the zone of play where a player is in an off-side position, they should whistle immediately and not await the outcome of the pass.
> Law 11 (c).

The European Union of Football Associations issued an instruction in 1971 to international Referees officiating in their competitions, that, 'the moment of the ball being released is in all cases decisive for off-side position and a decision must, therefore, be taken immediately by the Referee.'
When the Football League issued their 'Advice to Referees' in 1971 they included a statement on off-side interpretation as follows:

> *Off-side* (a) Referees must be satisfied that a player who is in an off-side position is interfering with play or seeking to gain an advantage before he penalizes him for being off-side.

(b) Linesmen should not 'flag' automatically if a player is in an off-side position. Before indicating to the Referee that a player is off-side the Linesman should ensure that the player is interfering with play or seeking to gain an advantage and should only 'flag' when he is satisfied that this is so.

(c) Having decided that a player is, in fact, off-side the Referee should blow his whistle immediately and not await the result of the pass. If, however, the ball touches, or is played by an opponent, whilst he is going to blow his whistle (but has not already done so), he should not blow it. (The action of the ball touching or being played by an opposing player brings into effect the 'unless' clause and Referees are not entitled to ignore it).

104 Is a player judged to be off-side if he is in an off-side position at the moment he receives the ball?

105 Is it an offence to be in an off-side position?

106 If a player at the taking of a goal kick is in an off-side position, should he be penalized?

107 Can a player be off-side in his own half of the field of play?

108 Is a player off-side if he is in line with the ball when it is passed to him by a colleague, i.e. the ball is the same distance from the goal line as the receiving player when the ball is passed?

109 Can a player be off-side if the ball was last touched by an opponent?

110 If an attacking player moves a little way beyond the
boundary of the field of play to indicate that he is not
interfering with play, does he infringe the off-side law?

111 May a defender step off the field of play in order to place
an opponent in an off-side position?

112 If a player, in an off-side position when the ball is played
towards him, moves into an on-side position, does this
place him on-side?

113 Is a colleague of the kicker allowed to stand in an off-side
position at the taking of a penalty-kick?

114 An indirect free-kick is awarded and the players
(defenders and attackers) line up on the goal-line
between the posts. A ball is deflected from an attacker
on the line into the net. What is the decision?

Laws 7-10

This section will deal with questions on the operational Laws of the Game (Laws 7-10), i.e. duration of the game, the start of play, ball in and out of play, and method of scoring.

115 Must a match be divided into two equal parts or is it permissible to have one half longer than the other, provided the total time is in accordance with the law, i.e. 90 minutes.

116 Has the referee power to add on time caused through accident or wastage?

117 If a match has to be abandoned by the referee (e.g. through inclement weather) before the completion of the time specified in the rules of the competition, can the score at the time of the stoppage be allowed to stand as the result of the match?

118 If the rules of the competition specify a certain length of time to be played, has the referee the power to decide otherwise, for example, may the time be reduced in the event of a late start and fading light?

119 What should be the duration of the half-time interval?

120 When does a match actually start?

121 At the beginning of a match may the captain winning the toss decide to kick-off instead of having choice of ends?

122 May a goal be scored direct from a kick-off?

123 If the ball is played backwards into the kicker's own half of the field at the commencement of a match, is this in order?

124 Under what circumstances is a match restarted by the Referee dropping the ball?

125 If the kicker at the commencement of the match plays the ball a second time before it has been touched or played by another player, is this an offence, and if so how is the game restarted?

126 If, when the Referee drops the ball, it goes over the touch- or goal-line before it is touched by a player, what action should the Referee take?

127 When extra time is necessary in a Cup Competition, which team kicks off at the start of such extra time?

128 If a player touches the ball before it reaches the ground when the Referee is restarting the game by the 'dropped' ball method, can play be allowed to continue.

129 If the Referee blows his whistle for the end of the first half of a match and the players leave the field and he then discovers he has played 5 minutes short, should he add this 5 minutes on to the second-half period?

130 How long should the interval be between the end of normal time and the start of extra time in a Cup Competition?

131 When kicking-off at the start of a match, a player miskicks the ball and it only travels a few inches, and the same player then kicks the ball again, is this an offence?

132 If it takes 5 minutes for the two teams to walk back to the dressing-rooms at the half-time interval, can the players insist on a further 5 minutes interval?

133 Is it necessary for the Referee to insist on an equal number of players from each side when he drops the ball for the restart of a match?

134 May a match be started by a person kicking-off who is not one of the players?

135 A shot from an attacker is about to enter the net but before it does a spectator prevents this otherwise certain goal, what is the Referee's decision?

136 What is the main purpose of the 'centre circle'?

137 Is there a maximum period of time that a match can be temporarily suspended, for say a cloud-burst, a crowd incident, failure of flood-lights, or other cause?

138 If the ball is kicked beyond the touch-line in the air and then re-enters the field of play, should the Referee allow the match to continue?

139 If two players of opposing sides strike or trip one another when they are outside the field of play and the ball is out of play, what action should the Referee take?

140 If the ball rebounds from the corner flag-post in to the field of play, should the match continue?

141 If the ball rebounds off either the Referee or a Linesman, should play be allowed to continue?

142 If the ball is entering the goal and a spectator encroaches and tries unsuccessfully to prevent it from so doing, should the Referee allow the goal?

143 A defender in order to save a certain goal punches the ball but only deflects it into the goal, should a goal be allowed or should a penalty-kick be awarded?

144 May a goal be scored direct from a throw-in?

145 If the ball strikes a half-way flag and rebounds into play, should play be allowed to continue?

146 May a goal be awarded if the goalkeeper throws the ball from his own penalty-area direct into his opponent's goal. (This would appear to be an almost impossible feat).

147 Is a neutral Linesman infringing the Laws of the Game if whilst the game is in progress he runs inside the touch-line on the field of play?

148 If the ball is accidentally propelled by hand or arm by a player of the attacking side over his opponents' goal-line, into the goal should a goal be awarded?

149 May a goal be allowed if the ball is clearly not going to enter the goal but is deflected accidentally by the Referee past the goalkeeper into the goal?

150 If a Referee inadvertently signals a goal in anticipation that the ball is going to enter the goal but it does not do so and he immediately realizes his mistake, is the goal valid?

Free Kicks

This section will deal with questions on free-kicks. Endeavours will be made to highlight the difficult and controversial incidents which do occur. Tactics arising from these situations in a match are very frequently well prepared and practised in the hope that goals may be scored. Many teams, from the most junior to those at international level, practise rehearsed moves at free-kicks near to their opponents' goal, corner-kicks and throw-ins.

The Referee, in judging infringements in connection with this section of the Laws, must always remember the Spirit of the Game.

Football Authorities have from time to time emphasized the importance of certain procedures at the taking of free-kicks. It may be interesting to quote an extract from Memorandum No. 5 of the Football Association, published in August 1951, and referring to a decision of 1910. These facts are equally applicable today.

'In order to carry out the spirit of the Law relating to free-kicks, Referees and players are reminded that there must be no undue delay in allowing the non-offending side to take a free-kick. This is especially so if the award is a direct free-kick. Unnecessary delay often means that inadequate compensation is made for the offence.

Law 13 in no way justifies a Referee allowing the side at fault ample opportunity to consolidate its defence; and it certainly does not relieve him from taking action against a player who purposely prevents the free-kick from being taken quickly or who does not at once retire to the proper distance (ten yards from the ball wherever possible). Such a player is committing a further offence and the Decision of the Council of December 1910 is still applicable:

Players who do not retire to the proper distance when a free-kick is taken must be *cautioned*, and on any repetition by *ordered off*. It is particularly requested of Referees that attempts to delay the taking of a free-kick by encroaching should be treated as serious misconduct.'

It may also be interesting to note that the following instructions have been issued by the Football League to its officials regarding the taking of quick free-kicks: 'Referees will allow quick free-kicks provided that the ball is correctly positioned. If a player takes a kick quickly and the outcome of the kick is not satisfactory to him he cannot then claim that the opposing players were not ten yards away.'

151 How many classes of free-kicks can be awarded?

152 When is the ball deemed to be in play at the taking of a free-kick?

153 At the taking of a free-kick, is an offence committed if the kicker plays the ball a second time before it has been touched or played by another player?

154 If the ball is 'rolling' when a free-kick is taken should the Referee take any action?

155 Is it necessary for the Referee to blow his whistle to signal the taking of free-kicks?

156 Are there any occasions when opposing players may be nearer than 10 yards from the ball at the taking of a free-kick?

157 When a free-kick is being taken from within the kicker's own penalty-area, an opponent enters the area and plays the ball after it has been kicked but before it has left the area. What action should the Referee take?

158 Is it permissible when a free-kick is being taken for any of the opposing players to gesticulate in a way calculated to distract their opponents?

159 A player kicks the ball directly into his own goal from
(a) a direct free-kick
or
(b) an indirect free-kick
Would a goal be awarded in either of these circumstances?

160 If a player kicks the ball from an indirect free-kick directly into his opponent's goal, what is the award and how should the game be restarted?

161 If a player taking a free-kick from outside his own penalty-area intentionally handles the ball after it has travelled the distance of its circumference and before it has been played by another player, he will have committed two offences. What are they and what is the punishment?

162 How would a goalkeeper be penalized for handling a ball outside his own penalty-area?

163 Is the 'donkey' type free-kick permitted, i.e. the kicker holding the ball between his feet and flicking it up in a backward direction for a colleague to attempt to score?

164 What is the signal given by the Referee to indicate an indirect free-kick?

165 May a free-kick be passed backwards?

Penalty Kicks

A penalty-kick is awarded for any of the nine penal offences committed by a defender in his own penalty-area, providing the ball is in play at the time the offence is committed.

166 Where must the goalkeeper stand at the taking of a penalty-kick?

167 May the player taking the kick pass the ball backwards for a colleague to run on to and score?

168 If a kick is ordered to be retaken for any reason, may a different player have the second attempt?

169 If the player taking the kick plays the ball a second time without its being touched by another player, what action should the Referee take?

170 If at the same time as the Referee blows his whistle to award a penalty-kick, normal time expires, would he permit the penalty-kick to be taken?

171 At the expiration of time a penalty-kick is being taken. Is the scoring of a goal nullified if the ball touches the goalkeeper before passing between the posts and over the goal-line?

172 If a defending player encroaches into the penalty-area or within 10 yards of the penalty-mark after the Referee has given the signal for the kick to be taken, but before the player has actually kicked the ball, what action should the Referee take?

173 If at the taking of a penalty-kick a colleague of the kicker encroaches into the penalty-area or within 10 yards of the penalty-mark before the kick has been taken, but after the Referee has given the necessary signal, what action should the Referee take?

174 If at the taking of a penalty-kick a colleague of the kicker encroaches and a defending player also encroaches, i.e. a technical infringement is committed by a member of both sides, what action should the Referee take?

175 If at the taking of a penalty-kick the ball rebounds from the cross-bar and the kicker then kicks it direct into the goal, should a goal be awarded?

176 If the pitch is in a waterlogged state and the penalty-mark is partly flooded, is the player allowed to place the ball elsewhere than on the penalty-mark?

177 May a player taking a penalty-kick pass the ball forward for a colleague to run into the area and score?

178 May a defending player go beyond the boundary of the field of play at the taking of a penalty-kick?

179 The Referee gives the signal for the taking of a penalty-kick, but before the ball is kicked he notices a colleague of the kicker encroaching into the area. He decides to allow the kick to be taken and the ball rebounds from the goalkeeper or the cross-bar into play. What action should the Referee take?

180 A player taking a penalty-kick may try to deceive the goalkeeper as to where he wishes to aim the ball. Is such action permitted?

181 A goalkeeper, in making a save, deliberately trips the oncoming forward and injures himself. What action should the Referee take?

182 May a goalkeeper be replaced by a colleague for the taking of a penalty-kick?

183 At the taking of a penalty-kick, if, after the kick has been taken, the ball is stopped in its course towards goal by an outside agent, should the kick be retaken or should the Referee drop the ball at the place where the interference occurred?

184 If, after a penalty-kick has been taken, the ball rebounds into play from the cross-bar and is then stopped in its course by an outside agent, what action should the Referee take?

Throw-In

F.A. MEMORANDUM No. 4   NOVEMBER 1949

THE THROW-IN. Law 15 states that 'the thrower shall deliver the ball from behind and over his head.' This implies that the throwing movement shall commence from a position over the head. Some officials have a mistaken impression that this phrase means that the ball must leave the hands when overhead. This is a physical impossibility unless the hands are checked in this position. A natural throwing movement starting from behind and over the head will always result in the ball leaving the hands when they are some slight distance in front of the vertical plane of the body. A player satisfies the condition of throwing if he starts the throw from over his head and the movement is continuous to the point of release.

Officials should not delay a throw-in. The side taking the throw-in should be able to take advantage of a quick restart of the game provided that it is in accordance with the conditions of Law 15.

185   The ball has been kicked out of play over the touch-line but before it is thrown-in a player deliberately kicks an opponent. What action should the Referee take and how should the game be restarted?

186   From a correctly taken throw-in, the ball does not enter the field of play after being thrown.
 What action, if any, should the Referee take?

187 Is it permissible for a player when taking a throw-in to have, at the moment the ball is released, one or both of his feet partially in the field of play?

188 If the thrower at a throw-in guides the ball with one hand and throws it with the other, as distinct from using both hands to throw the ball, is this a foul throw?

189 What is the Referee's decision if a player at a throw-in throws the ball direct into:
    (a) The opponents' goal?
    (b) His own goal?

190 If, when a throw-in is being taken, an opponent jumps up and down in front of the thrower in a way calculated to impede him, what action should the Referee take?

191 To save time a goalkeeper rushes out from his goal to take a throw-in. Is this in order?

192 If at the taking of a throw-in a player throws the ball on to the back of a passing opponent in order to gather the rebound, should this be permitted?

193 If a player correctly takes a throw-in and then plays the ball a second time before it has been touched by another player, is this permissible?

Goal-Kicks and Corner-Kicks

194 A goalkeeper taking a goal-kick kicks the ball out of the penalty area. The ball hits the Referee and rebounds into the goal. What should be the decision?

195 In similar circumstances to the previous question the ball strikes the Referee from the goal-kick and rebounds towards the goal. The goalkeeper, in a desperate effort to prevent the ball from entering the net, gets his fingers to it but nevertheless the ball crosses the goal-line between the goal-posts and under the cross-bar. What should be the decision?

196 If a player is intentionally tripped outside the penalty-area at the taking of a goal-kick before the ball has left the penalty-area, should a free-kick be awarded?

197 Where may the ball be placed for a goal-kick?

198 If at a goal-kick an opponent enters the penalty-area after the ball has travelled the distance of its circumference, but not left the penalty-area, and is then intentionally fouled by a defending player, what should be the Referee's decision?

199 A player, other than the goalkeeper, takes a goal-kick. The ball passes out of the penalty-area into play and is again deflected by the Referee back towards the goal. The player then plays the ball with his hand within the penalty-area. What should be the decision?

200 At the taking of a goal-kick the goalkeeper kicks the ball several yards into the opposing half of the field of play where a player of the goalkeeper's team is standing in an off-side position. He controls the ball and runs on and scores. Should a goal be allowed?

201 A goalkeeper taking a goal-kick sees that the ball will not reach his colleague standing at the side of the penalty-area, he therefore plays the ball a second time before it leaves the penalty-area. What action should the Referee take?

202 A goal-kick is taken and a member of the defending side steps into the penalty-area and kicks the ball back to his goalkeeper. What action should the Referee take?

203 May a goal be scored direct from a corner-kick?

204 A goalkeeper takes a goal-kick but before the ball passes out of the penalty-area an attacker runs inside to challenge for the ball. What is the decision?

205 A goalkeeper, from a goal-kick, kicks the ball beyond the penalty-area into play. It strikes the Referee and rebounds towards the goal, the goalkeeper plays the ball a second time but deflects it to an attacker who shoots into goal. What action should the Referee take?

206 Is it possible for a player to be off-side at the taking of a corner-kick?

207 May the kicker at the taking of a corner-kick move or remove the flag-posts?

208 How near to the ball may the defending players approach at the taking of a corner-kick?

209 If the player taking the corner-kick plays the ball a second time before it has been touched or played by another player, what action should the Referee take?

210 If the ball at the taking of a corner-kick rebounds from the goal-posts to the player who took the kick and he then plays it again, should the Referee allow play to continue?

The Last Question

211 In a schoolboy match an immigrant team of Indian boys were playing a team of English boys and one of the Indians, who was wearing a turban, caused the ball to be lodged in the turban. He then proceeded to run down the field towards his opponent's goal. Should the Referee have allowed him to continue or was he infringing a Law of the Game?

Answers

1 If: (a) in the opinion of the Referee he is guilty of violent conduct or serious foul play.
   (b) he uses foul *or* abusive language.
   (c) he persists in misconduct after having received a caution.
   (Law 12, paragraphs (n), (o), (p))

Note: A player may also be required by the Referee to leave the field if he is wearing any article that may be dangerous (either to himself, his colleagues or opponents) or which does not conform to the Law, e.g. a ring, or faulty or illegal studs; on occasions a plaster-cast covering an injured arm. In these instances, however, the player may of course return after remedying the fault and satisfying the Referee that everything is in order. (Law 4 refers)

2 If: (a) he enters or re-enters the field of play without having received the Referee's permission.
   (b) he persistently infringes the Laws of the Game.
   (c) he shows, by word or action, dissent from any decision given by the Referee.
   (d) he is guilty of ungentlemanly conduct, e.g. dangerous play, adopting an aggressive attitude, a foul tackle destroying a good advantage, hand ball preventing a goal being scored, etc.
   (Law 12, paragraphs (j), (k), (l), (m))

3 Award an indirect free-kick against the kicker for dangerous play. (Law 12)

4 Yes, if the Referee considers that it constitutes a danger to an opponent within the immediate proximity – an indirect free-kick would be awarded for dangerous play. (Law 12) (N.B. This 'dangerous play' must not be confused with the offence of 'kicking or attempting to kick', which is a penal offence.)

5   - (a) Kicking or attempting to kick an opponent.
     - (b) Tripping an opponent.
       (c) Jumping at an opponent.
       (d) Charging violently or dangerously.
       (e) Charging from behind unless the opponent be
            obstructing*
       (f) Striking or attempting to strike an opponent.
       (g) Holding an opponent.
     - (h) Pushing an opponent.
     _ (i) Handling the ball. (This does not apply to the
            goalkeeper within his own penalty area).
            It is important to remember that every one of
            these offences in order to be classified as a
            violation of the laws must be committed in an
            INTENTIONAL MANNER.
            A penalty kick can be awarded irrespective of the
            position of the ball provided that it is in play at the
            time an offence in the penalty area is committed.
            Law 12)
            *Charging an opponent from behind in the
             proximity of the shoulder in a reasonable
             manner should not be confused with charging
             in the back which is dangerous and must never
             be permitted.

6   (a) Dangerous play.
       (b) Charging fairly when the ball is not within playing
            distance.
       (c) Intentionally obstructing an opponent.
       (d) Charging the goalkeeper except when he
            (i)   Is holding the ball.
            (ii)   Is obstructing an opponent.
            (iii) Has passed outside his goal area.
       (e) The goalkeeper taking more than four steps
            whilst holding, bouncing or throwing the ball in
            the air and catching it again without releasing it

so that it is played by another player *or* time wasting. (Law 12)
(N.B. Time wasting must not be confused with time consuming i.e. when the goalkeeper can be legally challenged e.g. when dribbling the ball.)

7 Yes, provided the ball is in play when the offence is committed. (Law 12)

8 The player should be sent from the field of play and as the ball is not in play when the striking occurs the game should be restarted by the Referee again dropping the ball. A penalty kick should not be awarded. (Law 8, I.B.D. 1)

9 The player should be cautioned for entering the field of play without permission. The Referee should then punish the more serious infringement, which in itself may be a cautionable or a sending-off offence. (Law 12, Section (J))

10 He should send the player from the field. (Law 12, Section (p))

11 No. All cautions must be reported. (Law 5, Section (e))

12 A direct free-kick for holding, provided the ball is in play. (Law 12, Section (g))

13 Send the players from the field of play and recommence the game with an indirect free-kick against the offending side, at the place where the incident occurred, provided that the ball was in play at the time of the offence, and the offence took place within the field of play. (F.I.F.A. Q & A)

14 Presuming the goalkeeper was standing inside his penalty area a penalty kick should be awarded. (Law 12, I.B.D. 1)

15 The offence by the defender is obstruction and an indirect free-kick should be awarded against him. (Law 12, Section 3)
N.B. It may be opportune to quote an extract from an official F.A. Memorandum regarding obstruction.
F.A. Memo No. 4, November 1949
  Obstruction . . . is . . . opposed to the spirit of the game, where a player not in possession or within playing distance of the ball and without attempting to play the ball, intentionally moves to block or obstruct the path of an opponent who is trying to play the ball. Such actions are easily discernible from the natural obstruction which arises in the normal expression of the game. As there may be no attempt to charge on the part of the offender the infringement can only be penalized as ungentlemanly conduct and an indirect free-kick awarded.

16 Yes, but not in a violent or dangerous manner. (Law 12, 1BD 2) (Remember charging from behind is permitted in these circumstances and this is distinctive from charging in the back which is not permitted under any circumstances).

17 The Referee must judge the intention of the physical contact on the goalkeeper and shall only stop the game if, in his opinion, the physical contact by the attacker was made intentionally on the goalkeeper. An indirect free kick should then be awarded, if the contact was considered to be a fair charge, otherwise a direct free-kick should be awarded. (Law 12, Section 4)
An International Board Decision of the 25th September 1953 is also relevant:

In case of body contact in the goal-area between an attacking player and the opposing goalkeeper not in possession of the ball, the Referee shall blow his whistle for the foul if the action of the attacking player . . . was intentional. The Referee is the sole judge of this intention.

Many people think that Referees tend to protect the goalkeeper more than other players. This is not so. The fact is that the goalkeeper is protected under a certain clause in Law 12, where it is stated that he may not be charged unless he is:

(a) Holding the ball.
(b) Obstructing an opponent.
(c) Has passed outside his goal area.

18 No. This is classified as ungentlemanly conduct and an indirect free-kick should be awarded to the opposing side. (Law 12, I.B.D. 4)

19 This comes into the category of violent conduct and the offending player should be sent from the field. (Law 12, I.B.D. 13) The game should be restarted with an indirect free-kick to the opposing team provided the ball is in play at the time of the offence.

20 No.

21 The Referee should award a penalty because the handling offence took place within the penalty-area. (Law 12, Section (i))

22 The Referee should stop the play, dismiss both players from the field and recommence the match by dropping the ball at the place where it was when play was stopped. (Law 12, I.B.D. 11). (Law 8 Para (d))

23 Yes. An indirect free-kick would be awarded against the goalkeeper for ungentlemanly conduct. He shall also be cautioned. (Law 12, I.B.D. 12)

24 None. Play should continue. Only intentional hand ball is penalized. (Law 12, Advice to Referees)

25 If the Referee considers that the opponent was 'put off' by the shout (whatever the wording may be) he should issue a caution to the caller for ungentlemanly conduct. The game would then be restarted by an indirect free-kick. (Law 12, Section (m))
N.B. The fact that a player may prefix his shout by calling a colleague by name (e.g. 'OK, Bob, it's mine') does not alter the interpretation. There may be an opponent in the vicinity with the same name. If the Referee decides that the shout 'put off' the opponent then an offence has been committed.

26 Law 3, Decision 6 states that 'A substitute shall be deemed to be a player and shall be subject to the authority and jurisdiction of the Referee whether called upon to play or not. For any offence committed on the field of play a substitute shall be subject to the same punishment as any other player whether called upon or not.'
This means that a penalty-kick would be awarded. As entering the field without permission is a cautionable offence, the substitute would be cautioned and if the Referee considered that the hand ball constituted an act of ungentlemanly conduct, the substitute player may be barred from taking further part in the game. He would have been guilty of two cautionable offences, which means dismissal from the field. (Law 12, Decision 14)

27 Foul play is an act which, in the opinion of the Referee, is intentional and unfair and contrary to the Laws and spirit of the game, whereas dangerous play is an act which, in the opinion of the Referee, is intentional and fair but committed without due regard to the player's own safety or the safety of an opponent. It is accepted that foul play can be dangerous, but dangerous play is not necessarily foul.

Extract from F.A. Memorandum No. 4 from Law 12. Undoubtedly the application of Law 12, dealing as it does with fouls and misconduct, is of primary importance in controlling the game. So much depends upon the Referee's instantaneous judgement and his determination to adminster the law without fear or favour. The following are some of the most common criticisms directed at Referees which are relevant to this Law:

Intentional or Unintentional   Law 12 is quite emphatic that it is only the intentional offence which shall be penalized. It would seem that some Referees are taking the line of least resistance by awarding free-kicks and penalty-kicks whenever the ball strikes a player's hand or arm. Occasions do arise where it is impossible for the player to avoid handling the ball, having no time to withdraw his hand or arm before the ball strikes him. Such accidental handling contact should not be penalized, no matter in what part of the field it happens.

In the case of tripping it is not always easy to judge whether the tripping has been caused by lateness of tackle or whether it is intentional. If the Referee is convinced that the infringement is intentional he should penalize it, unless there is obvious advantage to the non-offending side by not so doing. A Referee should not allow such matters as the position where an infringement takes place in the field of play, an overwhelming goal lead to one side etc., to affect his decisions.

28 No. The Referee should only stop the game if, in his opinion, the player has been seriously injured. (Law 5, Section (g))
(The Football League have emphasized that a trainer should only be allowed on to the field to assess the injury of a player with a view to his removal from the field for treatment. A similar ruling was carried out with great success in the World Cup Final Rounds in Munich in 1974 and a considerable amount of time-wasting was avoided).

29 Yes. The Referee is in charge from the time he enters the field of play before the commencement of the match until after the termination of the match. 'His authority and the exercise of the powers granted to him by the Laws of the Game commence as soon as he enters the field of play.' (Law 5)
This authority continues during the half-time interval, both on the field of play and in the dressing-rooms. (Law 5, I.B.D. 4)

30 A direct free-kick outside the area. The International Board in 1967 decided 'that the offence or attempted offence is committed at the place where the player concerned initiates the action'.

31 No. Law 5 gives the Referee authority to caution or send off the field of play, players guilty of certain offences. For a limited dismissal system to come into operation the Laws of the Game would need to be amended and this can only be authorized by the International Board at its Annual Meeting. The International Board may authorize

Law amendments for experimental purposes for certain competitions.

32 No. The area behind the goal-line, whether it be in the back of the net or not, is off the field of play. The Referee would deal with the defender's infringement by sending him from the field and the game would be restarted by a 'dropped ball' from where the *ball* was when play was stopped, provided it was in play at the time. (F.I.F.A. Q & A)

33 No. The Laws of the Game provide that only the Referee may send a player from the field. (F.I.F.A. Q & A)

34 The player should be cautioned for ungentlemanly conduct and the game restarted by an indirect free-kick awarded to the opposing team from the place where the infringement occurred. (F.I.F.A. Q & A)

35 Yes, and the offender sent from the field. (F.I.F.A. Q & A)

36 No. The Referee should stop play and deal with the offending player. As the ball is not in play until it has passed beyond the penalty-area, the goal-kick should be retaken. (F.I.F.A. Q & A)

37 The Referee should deal with the defender for serious foul play, i.e. send him off the field and restart the game with a throw-in. (F.I.F.A. Q & A)

38 Award an indirect free-kick as the goalkeeper may not be charged whilst in his own goal-area unless he is holding the ball or obstructing an opponent. (Law 12, Section 4)

39 Provided the ball was in playing distance of both players and they were attempting to play the ball no offence has occurred and play should continue. (Law 12, Sections 2 & 4)

40 Yes. If the Referee considers the foul was sufficient to
    warrant the player being cautioned or dismissed from
    the field he should administer the caution or sending-off
    when the ball next goes out of play. (Law 12, I.B.D. 6)

The advantage clause in Law 5 states that the Referee shall
'refrain from penalizing in cases where he is satisfied that by
doing so, he would be giving an advantage to the offending
team'. This clause is basically applied in connection with
infringements against Law 12 (Fouls and Misconduct) and is
a most difficult aspect of refereeing. As has been mentioned
in the questions, a foul may be sufficiently bad to warrant the
issue of a caution but the Referee may decide that a definite
advantage is 'on' and allow play to continue and then issue
the caution at the next suitable opportunity. To take no
apparent action when an infringement occurs, and at the
same time maintain control, is the most difficult art that a
Referee needs to apply in order to become a better Referee.
Norman Burtenshaw, O.B.E., a former international Referee,
quotes the following situation which often occurs, and gives
a good example of advantage:

A forward is breaking through from the half-way line. The
opposition defence is outstretched. Only one defender is in
that part of the field. The defender closes, and realizing
that the forward has too much pace for him, he brings him
down. Both players are sprawled on the pitch.
As the Referee is about to blow for a free-kick, he notices
that the forward is showing signs of getting to his feet. The
ball is running clear. The forward could still reach it before
the goalkeeper races outside his area. What does the
Referee do? Does he give the free-kick at the point where
the incident took place, some dozen-or-so yards outside the

area? Or does he allow play to continue, in the belief that the forward could still score and would be penalized if play was brought back?

This is the kind of situation that is constantly facing Referees today. The Referee has only a split second to make up his mind. Under these circumstances if play is allowed to proceed and no goal results it is then too late to bring the game back to the original incident.

Many players acknowledge what the Referee is trying to do although his action doesn't always please the spectators. It is possible for a minute or so to elapse between the application of the advantage and the next stoppage in the game but the Referee still has the authority to caution or send off the offender.

Each game is different. Each game requires a different attitude of control within the Laws. Only the Referee has the feel of the game and knows how much advantage he can allow and how much advantage the players will accept. One important fact the Referee must keep uppermost in his mind in every game is that advantage must never be used at the cost of losing control.

Jack Taylor, O.B.E., who refereed the World Cup Final in Munich in 1974 considers that:

The most effective official is the unobtrusive Referee; therefore, whenever an advantage situation arises and the tempo of the game and the attitude of the players allows, the advantage should be used, thereby helping to create the unseen official, which benefits the players and spectators alike. However it must always be realized that control must never be sacrificed for advantage.

To say that physical play accounts for the more contentious incidents that occur in football is, I am sure, absolutely correct. Foul or unfair physical contact is the cause of more infringements against the Laws of the Game than any other type of incident or situation – it can cause retaliation and incites players and supporters. Even if physical contact involving *foul play* cannot be eliminated, it certainly must be very considerably reduced if football is to improve as a pleasurable activity and a major sporting spectacle.

The questions that have been included in this section illustrate the type of foul play that occurs too frequently and these infringements are sometimes the subject of official memoranda.
The following extracts from official memoranda highlight some important features which, when appreciated, give an indication of the difficulties confronting the Referee and prove that these problems have existed for many seasons.

F.A. Memorandum No. 4, November 1949

Charging A foul charge is deemed a major offence under Law 12 and is therefore penalized by a direct free-kick or a penalty if the infringement takes place in the penalty-area. Such fouls are charging in a violent or dangerous manner and charging from behind except when a player is obstructing.
An indirect free-kick is awarded against a player who charges fairly but at the wrong time. Such infringements are:
   (a) Charging the goalkeeper except when he is holding the ball, is obstructing or is outside the goal-area.

(b) Charging an opponent when the ball is not in playing distance and he is definitely not trying to play it.

Both (a) and (b) require further comment.

(a) Some Referees are inclined to give a goalkeeper absolute protection, even in a technical sense, by penalizing all contact with him. The law is quite definite on this point, in that fair charging of the goalkeeper is allowed if the goalkeeper has possession of the ball. Outside his goal-area a goalkeeper can be charged even if not in possession, provided that the charge is fair and both the goalkeeper and the opponent who is charging are within playing distance and attempting to play the ball.

(b) Charging an opponent fairly and at the wrong time should not be confused with obstruction where the player does not charge but interposes his body between an opponent and the ball. A player is not allowed to charge an opponent in order to let the ball run on to another player of his own side, nor can he charge an opponent to let the ball run out of play. In both cases he is not attempting to play the ball. A defender, therefore, is not allowed to deliver a fair charge on an attacker who is trying to charge a goalkeeper in possession of the ball because the defender is not making an attempt to get the ball.

F.A. Memorandum No. 5, August 1951

What constitutes the offence of obstruction?
During any match, in the ordinary course of play, there are many occasions when a player will come between an opponent and the ball, but in the majority of such instances this is quite natural and fair. He is intent upon playing the

ball and is entitled to make every legitimate move to obtain or retain possession of it. Provided that the ball is within playing distance the player may interpose his body between opponent and the ball in a feint to play at it and yet allow it to go to a colleague. This is again legitimate.

It is when the ball is *not* within playing distance of a player (say two or three yards) and when he is not making any attempt to play the ball that this offence *may* occur. But it is strongly emphasized, the offence *must* be *intentional*. It is quite possible for a player when not playing the ball to be in the path of an opponent and yet not be guilty of intentionally obstructing.

Common sense of officials in interpreting the spirit of the game will help to differentiate between incidents of obstruction which are fair and those which are intentionally unfair.

Football is a simple game and the principles of the laws and their interpretations continue season after season – the extracts taken from the two memoranda detailed above are basically as true today as they were when published in 1949 and 1951.

41 The field of play must be rectangular.
The length must measure between 100 yards and 130 yards and the breadth between 50 yards and 100 yards. The length shall in all cases exceed the breadth (in international matches it is necessary for the following measurements to apply.
Length 110 – 120 yards and Breadth 70 – 80 yards)
(Law 1 (i))

See Diagram *Page 26*

42 (i)   A to B .... 18 yards
    (ii)   B to C .... 44 yards
    (iii)   D to E .... 18 yards
    (iv)   F to G .... 6 yards
    (v)   G to H .... 6 yards
    (vi)   H to K .... 20 yards
    (vii)   N to J .... 12 yards
    (viii) J to M .... 10 yards

43 8 yards.

44 8 feet.

45 No. Goal-nets are optional. Many Competition Rules do,
however, state that goal-nets are essential in that
particular Competition.

46 The Law states that, 'The field of play shall be marked
with distinctive lines.' However, in the Advice Section it
is stated that in the marking of fields of play 'the
materials should not be dangerous, i.e. unslaked lime or
creosote.' Every endeavour should be made to comply
with this advice. (Law 1, Advice to Secretaries)

47 5 inches.
N.B. The goal-line shall be marked the same width as the
depth of the goal-posts and cross-bar. (Law 1, I.B.D. 4)

48 Provided the ball is in play when the offence is committed,
a penalty-kick should be awarded. (The space within
the inside areas of the field of play includes the width of
the lines marking those areas. I.B.D. 6, Law 1)

49 5 feet.

50 No. But if used they must be placed not less than 1 yard outside the touch-line. (Law 1, (2))

51 In a competition match, unless the cross-bar can be repaired or replaced so that no danger exists to the players, the match must be abandoned. In a friendly match, by mutual consent, a rope may be used as a substitute. (Law 1, I.B.D. 8)

52 Not more than 28 in. and not less than 27 in. (Law 2)

53 At the start of the game the weight shall be not more than 16 oz. nor less than 14 oz. (Law 2)

54 No. It is usual to play with a white ball under flood-lights and an orange or yellow ball on snow. (A green ball, of course, would not be suitable on grass.)

55 No. The whole of the ball must be over the whole of the line. (Law 9)

56 The Referee should stop play, obtain another ball, and recommence with a 'dropped ball' from the place where the ball burst, 2, (Law 2, I.B.D. 4)

57 Yes. Law 3 states that one of the players 'shall be the goalkeeper'.

58 There is no minimum number laid down in the Laws of the Game but the International Board is of the opinion that a match should not be considered valid if there are fewer than seven players in either of the teams. (Law 3, I.B.D. 2)

59 (a) Subject to various conditions and competition
     regulations, a team shall not be permitted to use more
     than two substitutes in any competition match. (Law 3
     (2))
     (b) In a friendly match, provided that agreement is
     reached, substitutes up to a maximum of five per team
     can be permitted. (Law 3 (3))

60 No. Once a player has been substituted he cannot take
     any further part in the game. (Law 3, I.B.D. 5)

61 No. Substitution must take place when the game is
     'stopped'. (Law 3, (5))

62 Provided the Referee indicates that the injured player
     may return he may do so whilst the game is in progress.

63 If a player (or a substitute player) enters the field of play
     without the Referee's permission he shall be cautioned.
     (Law 4, I.B.D. 6 and Law 12, Section (j) and Law 3 (5))

64 Yes. This is permitted but it is important that the Referee
     is advised before the change takes place. The change
     may only take place when the play has been stopped.
     (Law 3 (4))

65 It is now considered that if the goalkeeper changes place
     with a colleague without the Referee's permission, the
     two players would both be guilty of an act of discourtesy.
     Prior to a recent change in law the Referee would have
     awarded a penalty-kick as soon as the new goalkeeper
     handled the ball within his own penalty-area. The offence
     is now considered to be one of ungentlemanly conduct
     and the advice given to Referees is that at the first
     available opportunity, i.e. when the ball goes out of play
     (when the game stops), he shall caution both players

and then recommence the game as necessary, i.e. goal-kick, throw-in, free-kick, etc. (Law 3 (4) and Punishment (a))

66 The Referee shall be informed of the proposed substitution. The player who is to be replaced shall leave the field of play and the substitute shall then enter the field of play at the half-way line. The whole procedure must take place during a stoppage in the game. (Law 3, (5))

67 Yes. A further player (i.e. a named substitute) may take the place of the man ordered off but the referee shall not delay the commencement of the match. (Law 3, I.B.D. 4)

68 Yes, a team short of players may make up the number any time during the period of the match. (F.A. *Guide for Referees and Linesmen*)

69 He would stop the game and recommence the match. (F.A. *Guide for Referees and Linesmen*)

70 No. This would be considered part of a playing movement. Players are, however, expected as a general rule to remain inside the playing area. (F.I.F.A. Q & A)

71 He would decide if the 'protection' constituted a danger to the other players and if so, bar him from playing, unless he is able to remove the offending hazard. (Law 4, I.B.D. 4, and F.I.F.A. Q & A)

72 Yes. If, however, they are equipped with bars or studs these must conform with Law 4. (F.I.F.A. Q & A)

73 Yes, provided they conform to the requirements of Law 4, i.e. they shall be solid, the minimum diameter of any section of the stud must not be less than $\frac{1}{2}$ in., and the stud shall not protrude more than $\frac{3}{4}$ in. from the sole of the boot. Where metal seating for the screw type is used, this must be embedded in the sole of the footwear and any attachment screw must form part of the stud.
N.B.   It is important that nylon studs are inspected regularly, to ensure that no sharp edges constituting a danger to players are present. Studs which are moulded as part of the sole and are not replaceable may have a minimum diameter of $\frac{3}{8}$ in. (10 mm), provided that there are at least ten studs on each boot. (Law 4)

74 Yes. The International Board recently decided that in extremely inclement weather the Referee would grant permission for such equipment to be worn. (Law 4, I.B.D. 1)

75 Yes, if he considers it constitutes a danger. (Law 4, I.B.D. 4)

76 Yes, provided the Referee does not consider that the spectacles constitute a danger to the player or any of his colleagues or opponents. (Law 4, I.B.D. 4)

77 No. The Law states that the goalkeeper shall wear colours which distinguish him from the Referee. (Law 4)

78 Yes. Although this may not appear to be justice, this would be the situation. It must be remembered, of course, that the substitute could not be replaced by any other player. (I.B.D. 1971)

There are several questions in this publication concerning the use of substitutes. It may be of interest to note that the question of substitutes has been carefully considered by the International Board since 1939 and a Questionnaire to the eighty-seven member countries of F.I.F.A. was reported on at the International Board Meeting in 1957. Sixty-four countries had replied, forty-eight of which were in favour of substitution in one form or another. At the Board Meeting a proposal to permit an injured goalkeeper to be replaced in competitive matches was not accepted but the Board were of the opinion that consideration should be given to the possibility of Law change and at the Meeting in 1958 the following clause was approved:

> Substitutes for players injured during a match played under the Rules of a Competition will only be permitted if the approval of the National Association or International Associations concerned has been obtained.

Prior to this, substitutes for injured players were approved in friendly matches only.
In 1959, an additional phrase was added to the Law which said that the injured player must be 'unable to continue to play'.

For the Season 1965-66, in accordance with the Laws of the Game, the National Association, i.e. The Football Association, gave approval for one substitute player per team to be allowed because of injury for Football League matches only, as an experiment for twelve months.

For Season 1966-67, The Football Association approved the continuation of this experiment and gave permission for other Leagues to apply to implement this clause, and several Competitions took advantage of this.

For Season 1967-68, the F.A. Council agreed that approval be given for the use of one substitute in matches (no reference to injury) played under the jurisdiction of The Football Association. This followed the Change of Law which permitted substitutions of up to a maximum of two players per team, provided the authority of the International

Association or National Association was obtained.
The latest law change gives emphasis to the method of substitution and the fact that in friendly matches, provided that certain conditions are applied, up to five substitutes per team may be permitted.

79 Yes, he may insist that they keep a sufficient distance away from the perimeter in order to safeguard the players from possible injury. (Law 1, I.B.D. 12)

80 Yes. Law 3 states that a match shall be played by two teams each consisting of not more than eleven players . . .

81 He must ensure that nothing dangerous to other players shall be worn and, of course, that the colours of the two teams are distinguishable from each other and from those of the Referee. (Law 4)

This section among other things, dealt with the various dimensions of the playing-field, its appurtenances and the ball.
In schoolboy matches and women's football, various amendments are suggested to the dimensions quoted in the Law, e.g. smaller pitches, smaller goals and smaller footballs. This information can be obtained from Football Association publications (Referees' Chart and Know the Game).

82 (a) Enforce the laws.
    (b) Use advantage clause wisely (see Question 83).
    (c) Keep a record of the game and act as time-keeper.
    (d) Have discretionary power to stop the game, either temporarily or permanently.
    (e) Have the power to caution players and if they persist in further misconduct to send them off.
    (f) Allow no persons other than the players and Linesmen to enter the field without his permission.
    (g) Stop the game for serious injuries – arrange for slightly injured players to receive attention off the field.
    (h) Send off the field of play any player guilty of violent conduct, serious foul play or the use of foul or abusive language.
    (i) Signal for recommencement of the game after stoppages.
    (j) Approve the match ball.
    (Law 5)

83 No. He may refrain from penalizing in cases where he is satisfied that, by doing so, he would be giving an advantage to the offending team. (Law 5 (b))

84 No. He must send a detailed report to the proper Authority who alone have power to deal further with the matter. (Law 5 (d) and I.B.D. 9))

85 No. It is clearly stated in the Laws that the Referee shall not 'allow coaching from the boundary lines'. (Law 5, I.B.D. 12)

86 His authority and the exercise of the powers granted to him commence as soon as he enters the field of play. (Law 5)

87 He should punish the more serious offence. (Law 5,
    I.B.D. 10)

88 Only so long as the game has not been restarted. (Law 5,
    I.B.D. 5 & 6)

89 Only if a neutral Linesman can confirm that the goal was
    properly scored. (I.B.D., 10 March 1954)

90 Law 5, I.B.D. 11 states that, 'It is the duty of the Referee
    to act upon the information of neutral Linesmen with
    regard to incidents that do not come under the personal
    notice of the Referee.'
    I.B.D. 5 of the same Law clearly states however that, 'In
    no case shall the Referee consider the intervention of a
    Linesman if he himself has seen the incident, and from
    his position on the field is better able to judge.'

01 No, once having decided to play advantage the Referee
    cannot revoke his decision if the presumed advantage
    has not been realized. (Law 5, I.B.D. 7)

92 Yes. If the Referee considers that a caution or dismissal
    should be issued, the fact that an advantage has been
    played does not nullify this action. (Law 5, I.B.D. 7, and
    Law 12, I.B.D. 6)

93 The offence of striking has occurred and the Referee
    should send off the player and restart the game with a
    corner-kick because the ball was out of play when the
    offence occurred. (F.I.F.A. Q & A)

94 Yes. The players have a right to 5 minutes interval. (Law
    7, I.B.D. 2)

95 Yes. The League has this right and the Referee must reply, explaining the reason for his decision. (F.A. Referees' Committee, 1968)

96 The Referee should take on to the field of play the following items:
      2 watches (one which has 'stop' action)
      2 whistles, 2 pencils, note-pad/score card
      a coin and the match ball.
    (*F.A. Guide for Referees and Linesmen*)

97 No. The International Board has decided that the Referee for an international match must be chosen from the official list of international referees. (Law 5, I.B.D. 2 & 3)

98 In the event of undue interference or improper conduct by a Linesman, the Referee shall dispense with his services. An alternative official may then act as a substitute Linesman. (Law 6)

99 Flags should be supplied by the Club on whose ground the match is played. (Law 6)

100 No. When a team leaves the field of play without permission, the Referee has no option but to abandon the match. He must also, of course, report the facts to the appropriate Authority.

101 No. He may, however, inform the captain or manager of the team that the facts will be reported to the proper authority if the suspended player takes part in the match.

102 No. Once a player has been ordered from the field for misconduct he may not return.

103 Yes. Caution him for ungentlemanly conduct and if the
     game was stopped to issue the caution, recommence
     with an indirect free-kick. (Law 12 (m), and F.I.F.A. Q &
     A)

104 Not necessarily. The decision is made at the moment the
     ball is played to him. (Law 11)

105 No. Unless the Referee considers the player in the
     off-side position is interfering with play or with an
     opponent or seeking to gain an advantage. (Law 11,
     Punishment Clause)

106 No. A player cannot be off-side at the taking of a
     goal-kick. Nor can he be off-side at the taking of a
     Referee to restart a match. (Law 11 (d))

107 No. (Law 11 (a))

108 No. (Law 11)

109 No. (Law 11 (c))

110 No; unless the Referee considers that such a move is a
     tactical aim and the player quickly returns to the field to
     take further part in the game. (F.I.F.A. Q & A and
     I.B.D. 1934)

111 No. He would be guilty of an act of ungentlemanly
     conduct and should be ordered to return to the field of
     play. The Referee should allow play to continue and
     subsequently caution the defender. (I.B.D. 1934)

112 No. The Law (Law 11) states that off-side shall be judged
     on the player's position when the ball is last played. The
     Referee shall only refrain from penalizing the player if in
     the Referee's opinion he is not interfering with an

opponent, seeking to gain an advantage or if the ball is last touched or played by an opponent.

113 Yes. He may, however, be given off-side if the Referee considers that he is interfering with play or seeking to gain an advantage. (F.I.F.A. Q & A)

114 Off-side. As the players are level there are not two opponents nearer the goal-line than the attacker from whom the ball is deflected.

115 The game shall be two equal parts of 45 minutes, unless otherwise mutually agreed, i.e. the Rules of the Competition may permit reduced total time. In all cases, however, the two periods of play shall be of equal duration. (Law 7)

116 Yes, the amount of time added on shall be a matter for the discretion of the Referee. The Referee shall also extend time to permit a penalty-kick to be taken. (Law 7)

117 The match must be replayed in full unless the Rules of the Competition concerned provide for the result of the match at the time of such stoppage to stand. (Law 7, I.B.D. 1)

118 The Referee has no power to set aside the rules of the Competition regarding the amount of time to be played. (Law 7, Advice to Referees)

119 The half-time interval shall not exceed 5 minutes except by consent of the Referee. (Law 7)

120 When the player taking the 'place-kick' plays the ball forward into his opponents' half of the field of play for the distance of the ball's circumference. (Law 8)

121 The team winning the toss shall have the option of choice of ends or the kick-off. (Law 8)

122 No. (Law 8)

123 No. The match is not deemed to have commenced until the ball is played forward into the opponents' half for the distance of its own circumference. The Referee would order the kick-off to be retaken. (Law 8)

124 After any temporary suspension of play from any cause not mentioned elsewhere in the Laws of the Game, provided that the ball is in play at the moment when play was suspended. (Law 8)

125 Yes. It is an offence for the kicker to play the ball twice. In these circumstances an indirect free-kick should be awarded to the opponents, provided that the ball has travelled forward the distance of its circumference (27-28 in.) before it is played the second time. (Law 8)

126 The Referee should again drop the ball. (Law 8 (d))

127 The two captains should again toss for choice of ends or kick-off as they would at the start of the match. (Law 8, Advice to Referees)

128 No. The ball must touch the ground before it is in play. If this section of the law is not complied with the Referee shall again drop the ball. (Law 8)

129 No. He should recall the two teams on to the field of play and complete the last 5 minutes of the first half. (Law 7)

130 The length of the interval between the end of normal play and the start of extra time shall be at the discretion of the Referee. (Law 8, Advice to Referees)

131 No. The ball was not in play as it did not travel the distance of its circumference at the first kick. The kick-off should therefore be retaken. (Law 8)

132 No. At half-time the interval shall not exceed 5 minutes, unless the Referee so decides. (Law 7)

133 No. There is no obligation on the part of the Referee to insist on any particular number of players to be present at the dropping of a ball. (Law 8)

134 No. If it is a Charity Match and a ceremony is arranged for a local dignitary to take a kick at the ball, this is in order, provided the ball is brought back to the centre of the field and the kick-off is retaken by one of the players in accordance with the Law. (Law 8, I.B.D. 2)

135 A goal cannot be awarded if the ball has been prevented by any outside agency from passing over the goal-line. The game must be stopped and restarted by the Referee dropping the ball at the place where the ball came into contact with the spectator. (Law 10, I.B.D. 2), but this does not apply at the taking of a penalty-kick when under similar circumstances the kick would be retaken. (Law 14, 2 (a))

136 Opposing players must remain at least 10 yards from the ball until the kick-off has been taken, and the centre circle marks this distance. (Law 8)

137 No. This would be at the discretion of the Referee. In certain cases, however, where large crowds are present the Referee would appreciate advice and guidance from the Police and other Authorities. (Law 7)

138 No. When the ball has completely crossed the touch-line, whether on the ground or in the air, it is out of play. The Referee shall recommence the match by a throw-in. (Law 9)

139 The Referee shall take appropriate action against the players concerned, i.e. caution them or send them off. The game shall be restarted in accordance with the manner in which the ball went out of play. The restart may, therefore, be a goal-kick, corner-kick, throw-in etc. (Law 12, I.B.D. 11)

140 Yes. The ball would still be in play. (Law 9)

141 Yes, provided the ball is within the field of play when it strikes them. (Law 9)

142 Yes, unless the spectator made contact with the ball or in the Referee's opinion had interfered with play. In these latter circumstances the Referee would stop the game and restart by dropping the ball at the place where the contact or interference occurred. (Law 10, I.B.D. 3)

143 Provided the Referee had not blown his whistle for the hand-ball offence, he would allow the advantage and the score would stand. (Law 10)

144 No. If the ball is thrown direct by an attacker into his opponent's goal, a goal-kick would be awarded, and if a defender, when throwing the ball back to his own goalkeeper, throws it direct into his own goal a corner-kick would be awarded. (Throw means a throw-in, in accordance with the Law). (Law 10 and Law 15 – Advice to Referees section.)

145 No. The half-way flags are placed at least one yard
outside the field of play. The game would be
recommenced by a throw-in. (Law 9 and Law 1)

146 A goal would be awarded if this unlikely event occurred.
(Law 10)

147 In Law 9, Advice to Referees, it is stated, 'To prevent
being touched by the ball, or obstructing, Linesmen
should, as far as possible, keep out of the field of play,
although close to the touch-line.'
There may be occasions, however, when it is desirable
and helpful for the Linesman to run on the field of play,
i.e. cutting across the pitch from the goal-line after the
corner-kick has been taken, to regain his position on the
touch-line as quickly as possible. By implication, Law 5,
Section (f) indicates that the Linesmen may enter the
field of play, as this particular section clearly states that
the Referee shall 'Allow no person other than the players
and Linesmen to enter the field of play without his
permission'.

148 Yes. 'Intentionally propelled' is an offence. Accidentally
propelled is not an offence and a goal would be awarded,
provided no other breach of the Laws had been
occasioned by the attacking side. (Law 10)

149 Yes, provided the ball is in play when it strikes the
Referee. (Law 9)

150 No. The game should be restarted by a 'dropped' ball at
the place where it was it when the Referee incorrectly
stopped play. Under no circumstances may a goal be
awarded if the ball has not entered the goal. (F.I.F.A.
Q & A)

151 Two – Direct and Indirect. A 'direct' kick is one from which a goal may be scored direct against the offending side and 'indirect' is a free-kick from which a goal may not be scored unless the ball is played or touched by a second player before passing into the goal. (Law 13)

152 The ball shall be in play when it has travelled the distance of its own circumference *except* when the kick is taken from inside the kicker's own penalty-area. The ball shall then be classified as in play when it has travelled the distance of its own circumference and is beyond the penalty area. (Law 13)

153 Yes. An indirect free-kick should be awarded to the opposing team provided the ball has travelled the distance of its circumference at the time of the second kick and passed beyond the penalty-area if the kick was taken from within the kicker's own penalty-area. (Law 13)

154 Yes. It is essential that the ball is stationary when the kick is taken. The Referee would therefore order the kick to be retaken. (Law 13)

155 No. Provided a signal, either visual or audible, is given. (Law 5 (i))

156 Yes. (a) If they are standing on their own goal-line between the goal-posts, and
       (b) If the kicker indicates to the Referee, or it is obvious to the Referee that the player wishes to take a quick free-kick. (Law 13)

157 The Referee should stop play and order the kick to be retaken. (Law 13)

158 No. This would be deemed ungentlemanly conduct for which the offender should be cautioned. (Law 13, I.B.D. 3)

159 No. Law 13 clearly states that from a free-kick a goal can only be scored direct against the offending side. A corner-kick should be awarded in both cases, provided, of course, that in the case of a free-kick inside the penalty-area the ball had first been kicked into play. (Law 13)

160 No goal. The Referee should award a goal-kick. (Law 13, Advice to Referees)

161 He has played the ball twice and he has intentionally handled the ball. The hand ball is the more serious offence and the Referee should punish the offence by a direct free-kick or a penalty-kick if the offence took place in the player's own penalty-area. (F.I.F.A. Q & A)

162 By the award of a direct free-kick. (Law 12)

163 No. The International Board at its meeting in 1971 decided that this type of action is not 'kicking' the ball in the accepted sense of the word. (I.B.D. Q & A)
'Law 13 – Free-kick
In a match in England, in season 1970/71, a free-kick was taken in unorthodox fashion. The kicker made use of both feet in such a way as to 'lift' the ball into the air. The ball was directed towards a colleague who shot it into the goal. The Referee awarded a goal. In the view of the Scottish Football Association the ball was not kicked in the accepted sense of the word, and for this reason the free-kick was improperly taken, the goal should have been disallowed and the kick retaken. Is this view shared by the International Board?
The above question was put to the International Board by the Scottish Football Association and the Board shared the view of the Scottish F.A.'

164 The Referee, when awarding an indirect free-kick, shall indicate this by raising an arm vertically above his head. He shall keep his arm in that position until the kick has been taken. (Law 13, I.B.D. 1)
(It is recommended that the arm shall be maintained in the raised position until the ball is played by a second player or has passed out of play.)

165 Yes. The provisions of the Law must, however, be observed in connection with a free-kick from within the kicker's own penalty-area. (F.I.F.A. Q & A)
(This means that when the kick is taken by a defender from within his own penalty-area the ball must pass beyond the penalty-area before it is played or touched by another player.)
N.B. It should be remembered that apart from the 9 penal offences mentioned in Section 1 every other type of infringement for which the award would be a free-kick should be an indirect free-kick e.g.
Off-side
Carrying by the goalkeeper
Obstruction
Dangerous play
etc., etc. (Law 13)

166 The goalkeeper must stand (without moving his feet) on his own goal-line between the goal-posts until the ball is kicked. (Law 14)

167 No. The ball must be kicked forward. If this part of the Law is not complied with the kick must be retaken. (Law 14)

168 Yes. (F.I.F.A. Q & A)

169 The Referee shall stop play and recommence the game with an indirect free-kick to the opposing side from the place where the infringement occurred. (Law 14)

170 He must extend the time of play at half-time or full time to allow the penalty-kick to be taken. (Law 14)

171 No. A goal should be awarded. If, however, the goalkeeper parries the ball, thus clearly saving the goal, the Referee shall immediately blow his whistle for time. (Law 14, I.B.D. 6)

172 The Referee shall allow the kick to proceed but if a goal is not scored he shall order it to be retaken. The encroaching defending player shall be cautioned. (Law 14, 3 (c))

173 The Referee shall allow the kick to be taken. If a goal is scored it shall be disallowed and the kick retaken. The player encroaching shall be cautioned. (Law 14, 4 (b))

174 The kick if taken, whatever the outcome, shall be retaken. The encroaching players shall be cautioned. (Law 14, 5 (b))

175 No. The kicker has played the ball twice and an indirect free-kick should be awarded to the defending side. (Law 14)

176 No. The ball must be placed on the penalty-mark. (F.I.F.A. Q & A)

177 Yes, provided that:
    (a) All the players are in their correct positions at the taking of the kick.
    (b) The colleague to whom the ball is passed is not off-side when the ball is kicked.

(c) Provided that time has not been extended to allow the kick to be taken and all other requirements of the Law are satisfied. (F.I.F.A. Q & A)

178 No. All players must be on the field of play but outside the penalty-area and 10 yards from the penalty-mark, except of course the goalkeeper and the kicker. (F.I.F.A. Q & A)

179 The Referee shall stop play, caution the encroaching player, and restart the game by an indirect free-kick for the defending side. (F.I.F.A. Q & A) and (Law 14, 4 (c))

180 Yes. This is part and parcel of the game. If, however, the player stops his kicking action in order to make the goalkeeper move in one direction and then kicks it in the other or employs any other tactic that the Referee may consider unsporting, this is regarded as ungentlemanly conduct and is quite contrary to the spirit of the game. The player at fault should be cautioned and the kick retaken if a goal has resulted. (F.I.F.A. Memorandum, September 1969)

181 The Referee should award a penalty-kick, provided the incident took place within the penalty-area and the ball was in play. If the goalkeeper is injured he should receive treatment, if necessary.

182 Yes. Any player may change places with the goalkeeper at any time when there is a stoppage in the game, provided the Referee is advised. (Law 3, Section 4 & 5)

183 The kick shall be retaken. (Law 14, I.B.D. 2 (a))

184 The Referee shall stop play and restart it by dropping the ball at the place where the ball came into contact with the outside agent. (Law 14, I.B.D. 2 (b))

185 He should send off the offending player. The game is restarted by a throw-in. (F.I.F.A. Q & A)

186 As the throw-in has not been taken, i.e. the ball has not entered the field of play, the throw-in must be retaken. (F.I.F.A. Q & A)

187 Yes, provided that part of each foot is either on the touch-line or on the ground outside the touch-line. (His toes therefore can be within the field of play and his heels on the line or outside the line). (Law 15)

188 Yes, both hands must be used to throw the ball. (Law 15, I.B.D. 3)

189 (a) A goal kick.
(b) A corner kick.
(The Law clearly states that a goal shall not be scored direct from a throw-in). (Law 15)

190 If the Referee deems this conduct to be ungentlemanly the offender shall be cautioned. (Law 15)

191 Yes. Any player of the appropriate team may take a throw-in.

192 No. The Referee would deem such action to be ungentlemanly.

193 No. The ball has been played twice and an indirect free-kick should be awarded to the opposing team. (Law 15, Punishment Clause (b))

194 A corner-kick. Law 16 states that 'A goal shall not be scored direct from a goal-kick.'

195 An indirect free-kick against the goalkeeper for playing the ball a second time. (Law 16, Punishment Clause)

196 No. The ball is not in play until it has passed beyond the penalty-area. The goal-kick should be retaken and the offending player dealt with as necessary. (F.I.F.A. Q & A)

197 From a point within the half of the goal-area nearer to where the ball crossed the line. (Law 16)

198 The goal-kick should be retaken and the offending player cautioned or ordered off if necessary, according to the nature of the offence. (F.I.F.A. Q & A)

199 A penalty-kick should be awarded as the ball is in play before the intentional hand ball offence occurred. The player concerned has been guilty of two offences i.e. playing the ball twice at the taking of a goal-kick, and hand ball.
(Law 5, I.B.D. 10 states that 'If a player commits two infringements of a different nature at the same time, the Referee shall punish the more serious offence.')

200 Yes. It is not possible to be penalized for being in an off-side position at the taking of a goal-kick. (Law 11, Section (d))

201 Order the goal-kick to be retaken as the ball was not in play when the goalkeeper played it a second time, as it had not passed beyond the penalty-area. (Law 16)

202 Order the goal-kick to be retaken as the ball had not left the penalty-area and was not, therefore, in play. (Law 16)

203 Yes. (Law 17)

204 The goal-kick must be retaken as the ball was not in play when the attacker entered the penalty-area. (Law 16)

205 The International Board has decided that the Referee may either award an indirect free-kick for playing the ball twice or may apply the advantage and award a goal. This would be left to the Referee's discretion in accordance with Law 5, which entitles him to apply the advantage clause by refraining from penalizing in cases where he is satisfied that by so doing he would be giving an advantage to the offending team. This answer may sound rather contradictory, but the advantage clause is a matter for the discretion of the Referee and in these circumstances it would depend on whether at the time the ball was being played by the goalkeeper the Referee decided immediately to blow for the offence of 'playing the ball twice', or to allow a possible advantage as the ball landed at the foot of the attacker. (I.B.D., 1971)

206 No. (Law 11, Paragraph (d))

207 No. The corner-flags must not be moved or removed at the taking of a corner-kick. (Law 17)

208 The opposing players shall not approach within 10 yards of the ball until it is in play. (Law 17)

209 The Referee shall award an indirect free-kick to the defending team to be taken from the place where the infringement occurred. (Law 17)

210 No. The player has played the ball twice without its being touched by another player. (Law 13, Advice to Referees & Law 17)

211 This would be considered an act of ungentlemanly conduct and the Referee should stop the play, caution the guilty player and recommence the match with an indirect free-kick. [Could this happen? Would the referee caution? Think about it!!]

Conclusion

The Questions and Answers that have been posed in the foregoing pages have covered, as far as possible, the seventeen Laws that govern Association Football. There is one important aspect regarding the playing of the game which is not covered by law but is nevertheless included in the *Referees' Chart* and that is the section which lists the 'Instructions to National Associations and Continental Confederations' regarding the method of obtaining a result in a Knock-Out Competition.

In the Rules of a Knock-Out Competition, there are always regulations regarding drawn matches, extra time and replays. In many tournaments at the present time, Competition Rules decree that the system of 'Kicks from the penalty-mark' shall be used if a match is drawn at the end of full time or extra time.

It is not proposed to ask questions on this subject, as basically they would be technical questions of interest to the Match Referee concerned. It is sufficient merely to comment that this system has the approval of the International Board and is generally accepted to be preferable to the tossing of a coin. Referees officiating in matches which may require the 'Penalty-Kick' method should ensure that they are fully conversant with the procedures.

It is hoped that this book will have enabled the reader to appreciate the problems that confront the Referee in the modern game. It has already been mentioned that the Laws of Football are basically very simple and they have not been altered very much since those early days when uniform Laws were first agreed over 100 years ago.

In the early Laws adopted by the Football Association in December 1863, Law 10 stated that, 'Neither tripping nor hacking shall be allowed and no player shall use his hands to hold or push an adversary.' This general principle, of course, still applies today.

The memorandum extracts in this book, although in some cases originally written many years ago, are still very pertinent to today's game.

The difficulties confronting the present-day Referee, especially regarding control, are very much greater than they were a few decades ago.

Maybe this book will assist, in some small measure, in improving the standard of knowledge of the Laws of the Game for some enthusiasts which will in turn be of benefit to Association Football.

The indispensable argument settler
for every soccer enthusiast

THE REFEREES' CHART
AND PLAYERS' GUIDE
to the Laws of
Association Football

Revised and up-dated for the new season

An official F.A. Publication

40p

The essential reference book
for every soccer fan's bookshelf

THE F.A. YEAR BOOK
1976-77

Revised and up-dated for the new season

95p

Windows

THE POCKET REFERENCE

Allen L. Wyatt

Osborne **McGraw-Hill**

Berkeley   New York   St. Louis   San Francisco
Auckland   Bogotá   Hamburg   London   Madrid
Mexico City   Milan   Montreal   New Delhi
Panama City   Paris   São Paulo   Singapore
Sydney   Tokyo   Toronto

Osborne McGraw-Hill
2600 Tenth Street
Berkeley, CA 94710
U.S.A.

Osborne McGraw-Hill offers software for sale. For information on software,
translations, or book distributors outside of the U.S.A., please write to Osborne
McGraw-Hill at the above address.

Windows: The Pocket Reference

Publisher:	Kenna S. Wood
Acquisitions Editor:	Jeff Pepper
Copy Editor:	Ann Krueger Spivack
Indexer:	Sharon Hilgenberg
Typesetting:	Discovery Computing, Inc.
Cover Design:	Bay Graphics Design, Inc.
	Mason Fong

1234567890 DOC 9987654321

ISBN 0-07-881750-1

DEDICATION

To Debbie. For a disastrous day in April,
an exhausting weekend in May,
and an eternity of joy.

CONTENTS

Introduction

Windows 3 has been nothing short of a modern computing marvel. In just slightly over a year, Microsoft has sold millions of copies of their latest version of Windows, which has some appealing improvements over earlier, less powerful versions.

Windows is the graphical user interface (GUI) for DOS, an older and stodgier character-based interface for IBM-compatible personal computers. Windows 3 has opened the DOS environment to an ease of use previously unknown except to users of the Macintosh.

Why This Pocket Reference?

This pocket reference attempts to present the most commonly used Windows 3 commands in a manner that is clear, concise, and useful. In addition, near the back of the book you will find a *Task Reference*, a collection of common Windows problems and their solutions.

This pocket reference is not meant to replace larger, more complete books. Instead, it is meant to augment them. *Windows: The Pocket Reference* is designed to serve as a memory jogger or a quick reference. Its small size makes it convenient to carry it anywhere you need it.

Where do you look for more information than is possible to present in as short a volume as this? If you are interested in further information about Windows, the following books will definitely be of interest:

Windows 3 Made Easy, by Tom Sheldon, is a great book for beginners. If you are new to Windows, it will provide you with the solid basis you need to become proficient with the software.

Windows 3: The Complete Reference, by Tom Sheldon, is the most comprehensive guide to using Windows available. It provides all the help you will need to install, use, upgrade, and live with Windows.

If you also want to learn about DOS, the operating system used by Windows, then the following books are for you:

Simply DOS, by Kris Jamsa, is for the absolute DOS beginner. Written in a clear, concise manner, it provides an organized approach to the operating system in short, easy lessons. Packed with hundreds of pictures, this book is like no other on the market.

Teach Yourself DOS, by Herb Schildt, is for those a little more comfortable with computers, but unfamilar with using DOS. It provides a tried and true approach to teaching that will enable you to learn and grow at your own speed.

DOS: The Complete Reference, Third Edition, by Kris Jamsa, is the complete guide to DOS. This third edition of this classic provides the most comprehensive coverage of DOS of any book on the market.

All these books are published by Osborne/McGraw-Hill, and are available at bookstores everywhere. If you cannot find them at your bookstore, call 1-800-227-0900 for assistance in locating them.

Using This Pocket Reference

There are three sections to this pocket reference.
The first section gives information that is
fundamental to understanding Windows 3 and fully
absorbing the information in the other two sections.
If you are somewhat familiar with Windows,
however, you can probably skip the first section, or
just scan it.

The second section, the Command Reference,
presents the most commonly used Windows 3
commands in alphabetical order. Commands
included in the Command Reference come from the
following programs:

Control Panel

Program Manager

File Manager

Print Manager

Clipboard

Windows Setup

Control Menu

Commands are also included from the Help System. The Command Reference begins on page 17.

The third section, the Task Reference, presents common Windows tasks, again in alphabetical order. This section is provided for readers who may have a tendency to task-based learning as opposed to command-based learning. If you ever find yourself wondering "How do I do...," then this section will help you out. The Task Reference begins on page 151.

The beginning of each section explains how the commands and tasks are presented in that section; read the first several pages of each section to understand how to use the Command and Task References.

Finally, there is an index at the back of the pocket reference. Special care has been taken to make this index as complete as possible.

Keyboard commands presented throughout the book are presented in a different typeface and a different color. For instance, if you see the characters ALT-V-S, that means to hold down the ALT key, press V and then S. You don't have to hold down all three keys at once.

What Is Not Covered

While this pocket reference provides complete coverage of common Windows 3 commands, it cannot thoroughly cover an environment as rich, diverse, and powerful as Windows.

A conscious decision was made to focus strictly on the major commands that Windows users would encounter during day-to-day operations. Thus, this pocket reference does not cover information about the desk accessories and games that come with Windows. While these are powerful and useful programs, they are an adjunct to Windows, not a direct part of the system. Besides, to do those topics justice requires a larger-format book.

With all this in mind, let's jump right in.

Running Windows

Windows is a graphical user interface (GUI) that runs under DOS. Many people have their systems configured so that Windows begins every time they turn on their computers. Other people must explicitly start Windows each time they want to use it. This section is for the latter group of users.

The basic command for starting Windows is

```
WIN /x command /m
```

where **WIN** is the name of the program that contains the programming code for Windows, */x* is an optional mode switch, ***command*** is an optional startup command, and */m* is an optional memory switch if you are running Windows in real mode.

Notice that everything except WIN is optional; **WIN** is all you really need to enter in order to begin using Windows. However, you can use the mode switch (*/x* in the previous command line) to indicate the specific operating mode you want Windows to use. There are three operating mode switches, as follows:

/R   Real mode
/S   Standard mode
/3   386 Enhanced mode

Let's take a look at each of these operating modes.

Real Mode

/R tells Windows to begin in what is called *real mode*. This is an operational mode that makes the system work just like earlier versions of Windows. Some programs written for older versions of Windows will not work with the newer version. For instance, PageMaker 3.0 will not work with Windows 3 unless you use the /R switch.

When operating in real mode, you will not be able to access any extended memory that may be installed in your system. Real mode only uses expanded memory.

You also must use real mode if your computer uses an 8088/8086 CPU.

Standard Mode

/S forces Windows to operate in *standard mode*. This is an operating mode designed for systems that have a limited amount of memory, typically systems based on the 286 chip.

Still, your system must have at least 1MB of memory, meaning 640K of conventional memory and 256K of extended memory.

For many users, standard mode is the preferred operating mode for Windows. Because it does not allow multitasking (using multiple programs at the same time), the Windows software has to do less. This means that Windows takes less space in memory and consequently runs faster than 386 enhanced mode. While such a decision remains a personal preference, if you typically run only one application program at a time, you should try standard mode.

386 Enhanced Mode

/3 is the full-powered operating mode for Windows
3. With this switch, Windows uses *386 enhanced
mode*. In this operating mode, Windows can access
multiple programs, provide greater control for non-
Windows programs, and use the full capacity of the
higher-powered CPU chips.

To use this mode, your computer must have at least
a 386 chip and 2MB of memory. In 386 enhanced
mode, Windows uses all your available extended
memory.

Starting Without a Mode Switch

If you start Windows without the mode switch, it
will automatically determine which operating mode
to use after evaluating your hardware and memory.
Typically you will not need to use the mode
switches unless you need compatibility with older
software.

If you do not use the mode switches, you can
determine which operating mode is in use by
pulling down the Help menu from the Program
Manager. Select the bottom choice, "About
Program Manager...". When you do, a window
similar to the following will appear:

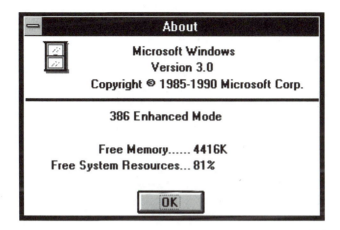

The Startup Command

The next part of the Windows command line is the
Startup command. You may use this command
immediately after starting Windows—for instance to
go directly into a Windows application such as
Excel. To do so, you would enter a line such as this:

```
WIN EXCEL.EXE
```

This assumes, of course, either that the program
EXCEL.EXE is available in the directory from which
you are running Windows, or that it can be found by
way of your search path. If not, then you will need
to include the complete path for the Windows
program in the command line. For instance, if
Windows was installed in the WIN3 subdirectory on
the D: drive, you could enter the following from any
subdirectory:

```
D:\WIN3\WIN EXCEL.EXE
```

The Real-Mode Memory Switches

The last thing covered here are the optional memory switches. These switches are only applicable if you are using Windows in real mode. If you are running Windows in standard or 386 enhanced mode, they have no effect.

There are three possible memory switches: /E, /L, and /N. Let's take a very cursory look at them. (A full exploration of memory use and switches could take an entire book by itself, and is beyond the scope of this pocket reference.)

/E controls how Windows uses conventional memory for expanded memory frame buffers. You should include a number immediately after /E (with no intervening space) to indicate the amount of conventional memory necessary before Windows should use large-frame mode.

/L, followed immediately by a positive or negative number, informs Windows how to move the expanded memory bank line. This switch only has effect if using large-frame EMS mode.

/N causes Windows to not use EMS at all.

The Windows Environment

If you are familiar with the character-oriented world of DOS, then working with Windows may be quite foreign to you. Basically, a character-oriented user interface is centered around words and commands. A graphical user interface, like Windows, is centered around pictures and menus.

When you start Windows, you are presented with what is referred to as the *desktop*. This is the screen area around which you can move graphic items, much as you would move items on your desk. The two types of graphic items are called *windows* and *icons*. Windows represent work areas, and icons represent files, including programs and data.

Here is what a typical desktop looks like, right after starting Windows:

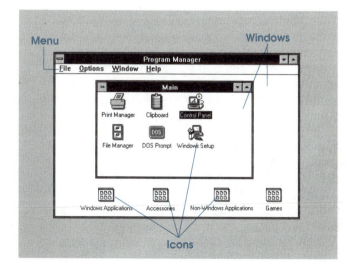

Windows

There are two types of windows: *application windows* and *document windows.* Application windows are created by Windows for programs currently running, and document windows are created by the individual applications. An easy way to tell the two apart is to remember that application windows have menus, while document windows do not.

In the illustration you just saw of the desktop, the window titled Program Manager is an application window, while the window titled Main is a document window. Document windows always occur within application windows; they cannot be moved out of them.

Icons

Take another look at the Windows desktop. Notice the tiny pictures or *icons.* These icons are graphic representations of programs. You can move them around your desktop, if you want, but they must remain in the window in which they exist. For instance, the icon titled Games cannot be moved outside of the Program Manager window.

The icons at the bottom of the screen, which are contained within the Program Manager window, are graphic representations of *program groups.* This is a special type of icon that indicates that there are other programs and files within that icon. When you open one of these icons, you will see a document window containing other programs.

For instance, the window titled Main contains a group of application programs—it is a program group. If this window were closed, it would look like the other icons at the bottom of the Program Manager window, except that the text under the icon would say Main.

Menus

Application windows have *menus* in them. These menus appear as a series of words under the application window title. You can access these windows by using either the keyboard or the mouse; both methods will be covered in more detail over the next couple of pages.

In the sample Windows desktop shown on page 11, the available menu choices are File, Options, Window, and Help. These are the menu choices for the Program Manager application; this is why they are within the Program Manager window. The choices available on menus are determined by the application program. There is no standard for what they contain.

Besides the application menus, there is another menu you need to be aware of. This is the *Control menu*, and it appears as an icon in the upper-left corner of every window. The icon looks like this:

When you activate this menu, you bring up a special set of choices that affect either the entire window or the entire application. Unlike application program menus, the commands available from this menu are standardized. While the Control menu for applications windows differs slightly from that for document windows, the functions provided by the Control menu are consistent throughout Windows.

Again, this menu can be accessed either by keyboard or mouse. The commands available from this menu are included in the Command Reference portion of this pocket reference.

Using the Keyboard

There are two ways you can give commands in Windows. You can use the keyboard or a mouse; for most actions the mouse is easiest. The mouse allows you to point at an object (such as a window, a menu, or an icon) and take some action on the object. Throughout this pocket reference you will see operations presented for both types of users: keyboard and mouse.

If you are using a keyboard, you begin most commands by holding down either the ALT or CTRL keys. You follow this by pressing a key that activates a menu, and then a key that activates a choice on that menu. Notice on the desktop presented earlier the several menu commands: File, Options, Window, and Help. Each of these has a single letter underlined. In this instance it is the first letter of each word. Note that it is not necessarily the first letter. In many cases the second or third letter indicates the key you want to press. You will have to look at the menu choices to verify which mnemonic key is used for a given menu command.

To access the Help menu, you use the key combination ALT-H. You can press both keys at the same time, but it is not necessary. Pressing ALT

activates the menu bar, and the next key you press
indicates which menu you want. In this case,
pressing the letter H indicates you want the Help
menu. When this is done properly, the Help menu
appears as shown here:

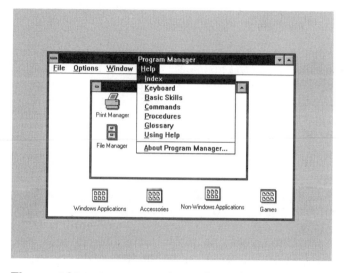

The next key you press selects the menu command
you want. There is no need to press ALT again. If
you do, the menus go away and you will need to
start over. Simply press the underlined letter.
Thus, if you want to access the command Using
Help from the keyboard, the entire key sequence is
ALT-H-U.

By the way—you can access the Help System any
time you are stuck in Windows. It is a powerful
system that will come to your aid in many
situations.

Using the Mouse

If you are using a mouse, most commands are started by clicking or double-clicking on an object. *Clicking* means pressing the left mouse button once. *Double-clicking* means pressing the left mouse button twice in quick succession.

For instance, if you wanted to access the Help menu mentioned in the last section, all you need do is click once on the word "Help," and click again on the words "Using Help." In two quick movements you have let Windows know exactly what you want to do.

What about double-clicking? A common example would be opening and closing windows. Looking at your desktop, if you double-click on a program group icon within the Program Manager (such as Main, Accessories, or Games), the icon would expand to an open window. If you then double-click on the Control Menu icon in the upper-left corner, the window will close, returning to a single icon.

Throughout this pocket reference you will see instructions to click or double-click. You will also see instructions to *drag* an item. Dragging means to point to an item, click on it, and move the mouse while holding down the left button. In this way you can move things around on the screen.

Command Reference

This section provides a quick overview of the commands available in Windows 3. Because Windows is a *menu-driven* program, a command is basically an option available from one of the many menus in Windows. Thus, each of the commands presented in this section represents a menu choice you can make.

The commands are arranged in alphabetical order, regardless of the Windows application that uses them. All commands use the following format:

COMMAND NAME

Program Name

The command heading shows the command name and directly underneath is the program to which the command is applicable. These include commands from the Control Menu, Program Manager, Control Panel, File Manager, Print Manager, Clipboard, Setup, and the Help System. If the command applies to more than one program, then both program names are given under the heading.

If the command is available system-wide, meaning it can be accessed through the Control menu, then the program is shown simply as *System-wide*.

Following the program name is a concise, one- or two-line description of what the command does.

Menu Structure

The first category after the command name is *Menu Structure*. This section indicates the series of menus you must follow, once within the correct program for that command, in order to access the command.

Steps

The next category is *Steps*. This section tells you how you can quickly invoke the command, once you are using the program from which the command can be used. The keyboard line tells you how to call up the command directly from the keyboard. The shortcut line indicates which keys (if any) can be used instead of the keyboard command. Finally, the mouse line tells you how to access the command with the mouse; this typically involves clicking on several menu selections.

Notes

The *Notes* category describes what the command does, along with any important considerations in using the command, and also gives you related commands. For most readers, this section will provide the most pertinent information.

Tips

Last is the optional *Tips* category. This section gives hints and warns against any "gotchas" that should be kept in mind while using the command.

There are 93 commands in this part of the pocket reference. (There are 98 commands in the following list because some, such as Cascade Windows, exist under several programs so are listed more than once here.) Following this list, the commands are arranged in alphabetical order. If you don't know the name of the command you need, try the next section, the Task Reference, which is organized by task.

Since this section of the book gives *all* of the commands in alphabetical order, the following list lets you see under which program each command falls:

Program	Command Name
Clipboard	Delete Clipboard
	Open Clipboard File
	Save As
Control Panel	386 Enhanced Settings
	Color Settings
	Date & Time Settings
	Desktop Settings
	Font Settings
	International Settings
	Keyboard Settings
	Mouse Settings
	Network Settings
	Port Settings
	Printer Settings
	Sound Settings
File Manager	Associate File
	Cascade Windows
	Change Attributes
	Close All Directories
	Collapse Branch
	Confirmation Options

Program	Command Name
File Manager (*continued*)	Connect Net Drive
	Copy Diskette
	Copy File
	Create Directory
	Delete
	Deselect All
	Disconnect Net Drive
	Expand All
	Expand Branch
	Expand One Level
	Format Diskette
	Label Disk
	Lower Case
	Make System Diskette
	Minimize on Use
	Move File
	Open
	Print File
	Refresh
	Rename
	Replace on Open
	Run
	Search for Files
	Select All
	Status Bar
	Tile Windows
	View By Name
	View By Type
	View File Details
	View Include
	View Name
	View Other
	View Sort By

Program	Command Name
Help System	Annotate
	Back
	Browse Backwards
	Browse Forwards
	Copy
	Define Bookmark
	Index
	Open File
	Print Topic
	Printer Setup
	Search
Print Manager	Alert Always
	Flash if Inactive
	High Priority
	Ignore if Inactive
	Low Priority
	Medium Priority
	Network Options
	Other Net Queue
	Selected Net Queue
	Update Net Queues
Program Manager	Arrange Icons
	Auto Arrange
	Cascade Windows
	Copy Program Item
	Delete
	Exit Windows
	Minimize on Use
	Move
	New
	Open

Program	Command Name
Program Manager (*continued*)	Properties Run Tile Windows
Setup	Change System Settings Set Up Applications
System-wide	Close Window Maximize Window Minimize Window Move Window Next Window Restore Window Size Window Switch To

386 ENHANCED SETTINGS

Control Panel

This command controls how non-Windows programs function in the multitasking Windows environment.

Menu Structure

386 Enhanced

Settings | 386 Enhanced...

Steps

Keyboard: Alt - S - 3
Shortcut: None
Mouse: Click on Settings menu, then click on 386 Enhanced...; or double-click on the 386 Enhanced icon

Notes

This command is only available if you are running Windows in 386 enhanced mode. If you are not, then the icon will not be visible on the control panel or on the Settings menu.

There are two types of 386 Enhanced Settings: those dealing with *device contention*, and those dealing with *scheduling*. Device contention has to do with how the system handles simultaneous requests for access to the serial and parallel ports by non-Windows applications. Only conflicts between non-Windows applications are affected by these settings; conflicts between Windows applications are dealt with directly by Windows. The three settings governing contention resolution are

Always Warn   This setting causes the display of a warning message when a conflict occurs. With the Always Warn setting, every time there is a conflict, you decide who gets access.

Never Warn   Don't ask; ignore the conflict and use the port. The Never Warn setting may result in more than one application using the same port at the same time, thus resulting in scrambled data being sent to the serial or parallel port.

Idle   This setting represents an idle time, in seconds, that indicates how long the port should remain idle before switching to another use.

Scheduling settings govern how Windows does multitasking when one of the tasks being executed is a non-Windows program. Here you can specify the amount of time devoted to running Windows applications when the foreground task is a non-Windows program, as well as the amount of time dedicated to running non-Windows programs when they are in the background. The time values set represent percentages of the total CPU time.

Tips

Typically the default values are sufficient for most needs. If you find yourself using a lot of non-Windows applications, make some adjustments to see if your overall processing speed improves.

ALERT ALWAYS

Print Manager

The Alert Always command allows the Print Manager to inform you as soon as it detects an error in printing.

Menu Structure

Options | Alert Always

Steps

Keyboard: Alt-O-A
Shortcut: None
Mouse: Click on Options menu, then click on
              Alert Always

Notes

The Print Manager governs how Windows interacts with your printer. It is a spooling utility, and its use is completely optional. Since printers are usually slower than computers, a spooling utility (such as the Print Manager) allows information to be sent to your printer at the speed your printer can accept it, freeing up your computer to work on other tasks.

This is a toggle option, meaning that you use the same command to turn the option on and off. When you select the command the first time, the error notification status for the Print Manager is changed, and a check mark appears beside the command on the menu. If you use another error notification command (Flash if Inactive or Ignore if Inactive), the check mark moves to the other command setting.

Typically the work done by the Print Manager is not done in an active window. It is usually done in the background while you are concentrating on other, more pressing tasks. Using this command causes the Print Manager to display a dialog box whenever it detects a printer condition that demands your attention. This dialog box appears regardless of what you are working on at the time, and allows for the fastest turnaround and most urgency when dealing with printing jobs.

This command is often used if the printer you are using is not near your computer. For instance, if you are printing to a network printer in another office, you may want to be alerted when problems occur.

Tips

If you find dealing with unexpected dialog boxes to be distracting, use one of the other two notification commands (Flash if Inactive or Ignore if Inactive) to set what you feel is appropriate.

ANNOTATE

Help System

The Annotate command allows you to add your own text to the Help System.

Menu Structure

Edit | Annotate...

Steps

Keyboard: ALT-E-A
Shortcut: None
Mouse: Click on Edit menu, then click on
Annotate

Notes

While the Help System built into Windows is
extensive, sometimes you discover additional tips,
tricks, and secrets that need to be kept in a central
place. This command allows you to expand the text
within the Help System.

When you use this command, you are presented
with a window in which you can type anything you
want. What you type is called an *annotation*, and is
added to the Help System section you were in while
you typed it. Those sections with annotations are
indicated by a Paper Clip icon to the left of the
section name. When you click on the Paper Clip
icon, you are shown the annotation.

Please note that you cannot place annotations at
random places throughout the text. They are
grouped with major sections and automatically
placed next to the topic heading.

Tips

You can easily delete any annotation when you find
you no longer need it. Simply pull up the annotation

by clicking on the Paper Clip icon, and then click on the Delete button.

ARRANGE ICONS

Program Manager

The Arrange Icons command organizes the icons in the current window in an orderly fashion.

Menu Structure

Window | Arrange Icons

Steps

Keyboard: Alt-W-A
Shortcut: None
Mouse: Click on Window menu, then click on Arrange Icons

Notes

This command simply grabs all the icons in the current window and organizes them so they are placed left to right, as wide as the current window will allow. If there are more icons than can fit in one row, then additional rows of icons are created.

Icons are not placed in any specific order; they are simply "tidied up."

Tips

Spacing between icons can be controlled through use of the Desktop Settings command.

ASSOCIATE FILE

File Manager

The Associate File command allows you to associate files that have specific filename extensions with an application program.

Menu Structure

File | Associate...

Steps

Keyboard: Alt-F-A
Shortcut: None
Mouse: Click on File menu, then click on Associate...

Notes

Windows allows you to associate files having a common extension with a specific application program. This association informs Windows of the program it should run if you attempt to open a file that has that extension.

For instance, files with the extension TXT are
associated with the Notepad accessory. This means
that if you attempt to open a file with an extension
of TXT, Windows will automatically run Notepad
and load the file.

This feature is very powerful. With it, you can train
Windows to automatically treat most of your files
the way you want them treated. Windows comes
already set for the following associations, all related
to built-in desk accessories:

File Extension	Associated Program
CAL	Calendar accessory
CRD	Cardfile accessory
TRM	Terminal accessory
TXT	Notepad accessory
PCX	Paintbrush accessory
BMP	Paintbrush accessory
WRI	Write accessory
REC	Recorder accessory

When you install other Windows programs, these
automatic associations get updated. For instance, if
you install Excel, files with the extensions XLS,
XLC, XLM, XLW, and XLM are automatically
associated with Excel.

If you attempt to open a file that is not associated
with an application, you will get an error message.

When you choose the Associate command, you are
shown the document type (the file extension) and

prompted to enter a program name. Enter the full program name, including any drive and path name. You should also include the extension of the program (typically EXE).

If you choose the Associate command for a document type that has already been associated with a program, you are shown the current link. You can either change the link, or break the association entirely by erasing the program name.

You can view documents that are associated with files through use of the View Include command. See that command for more information.

Tips

When working in the File Manager, you can easily tell if a particular document file is already associated with a program file by looking at the icons. If it is associated, the icon for the document file looks different from that of non-associated documents:

Non-associated documents

Associated documents

Take a look at your most frequently used document files. If they have a common file extension, then you can use the Associate File command to associate them with the program that uses them. That way, you can browse through the files using the File Manager and have the proper program loaded automatically when you open the file.

AUTO ARRANGE

Program Manager

The Auto Arrange command instructs Windows to automatically arrange icons in a window that has been resized.

Menu Structure

Options | Auto Arrange

Steps

Keyboard: Alt-O-A
Shortcut: None
Mouse: Click on Options menu, then click on Auto Arrange

Notes

This is a toggle option, meaning the same command turns the option on and off. When you select the command the first time, auto arrangement is activated and a check mark appears beside the command on the menu. Select Auto Arrange again, and auto arrangement is turned off and the check mark disappears.

If auto arrangement is enabled, Windows will automatically rearrange icons when a window is resized.

Tips

If you don't want your icons rearranged every time
you resize a window, turn off Auto Arrange, and use
the Arrange Icons command when you want them
arranged.

BACK

Help System

A button in the Help System that moves you back to
the previously displayed Help System screen.

Menu Structure

Steps

Keyboard: ALT-B
Shortcut: None
Mouse: Click on Back button

Notes

The Help System built into Windows is very
powerful. It displays information from a help file in
a consistent and clear manner. These help files
have the HLP file extension. If, when loading an
application program, Windows discovers that there

is a help file that has the same root filename as the application program, that help file is opened and ready for use.

When you use the Help System, every display action you take using the display buttons (Index, Browse Backwards, and Browse Forwards) is remembered by the system. The Back command button allows you to step backward through your use of those display buttons. Thus, you go back one screen at a time in reverse order until you reach the screen that appeared when you first accessed the Help System.

The Back command button is not available when there is no previous screen to display. Also, the system does not remember your actions if you use the scroll bar on the right side of the help window. It only remembers screens displayed using the display buttons.

Tips

If you need to go back more than a couple of screens, either hold down the Browse Backwards button, or click on the Index button. Using the Index button will return you to the beginning of the current Help System file.

BROWSE BACKWARDS

Help System

A button in the Help System that displays the major help section just prior to the current section.

Menu Structure

Steps

Keyboard: ALT-R
Shortcut: None
Mouse: Click on Browse Backwards button

Notes

The Help System built into Windows is very powerful. It displays information from a help file in a consistent and clear manner. These help files have the HLP file extension. If, when the Help System is started, Windows discovers there is a help file that has the same root filename as the active application program, that help file is opened and ready for use.

This command allows you to step backward, one major topic at a time, until you reach the beginning of the help file you're currently viewing. It only displays the major headings, not individual screens of data. If the major topic on the screen is the first major topic in the help file, then the Browse Backwards command button is not available.

Tips

Generally the Index is the first major topic in a help file. If you want to jump to the beginning of a help file, use the Index command.

BROWSE FORWARDS

Help System

A button in the Help System that displays the next major help section in the Help System file you're currently viewing.

Menu Structure

Steps

Keyboard: Alt-O
Shortcut: None
Mouse: Click on Browse Forwards button

Notes

The Help System built into Windows is very powerful. It displays information from a help file in a consistent and clear manner. These help files have the HLP file extension. If, when loading an application program, Windows discovers that there is a help file that has the same root filename as the application program, that help file is opened and ready for use.

This command allows you to step forward, one major topic at a time, until you reach the end of the current help file. It only displays the major headings, not individual screens of data. If the major topic on the screen is the last major topic in the help file, then the Browse Forwards command button is not available.

Tips

If you are searching for annotations you may have made in the current help file, you can use this command to move to the top of each major section. If you see a Paper Clip icon to the left of the section heading, then annotations are available for that section.

CASCADE WINDOWS

Program Manager or File Manager

The Cascade Windows command arranges open windows in an overlapping fashion.

Menu Structure

Window | Cascade

Steps

Keyboard: Alt-W-C
Shortcut: Shift-F5
Mouse: Click on Window menu, then click on Cascade

Notes

Your Windows desktop can become more and more cluttered as new windows are opened. This can make your work more difficult. When you use this command, Windows rearranges the windows so they overlap, making them easier to view and work with.

When cascading windows, they are automatically resized and, if Auto Arrange is enabled, the icons are rearranged in each window. The following shows a sample screen after cascading:

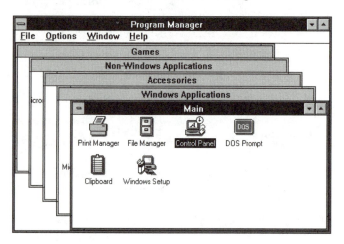

CHANGE ATTRIBUTES

File Manager

The Change Attributes command changes the properties assigned to a file.

Menu Structure

File | Change Attributes...

Steps

Keyboard: ALT-F-G
Shortcut: None
Mouse: Click on File menu, then click on Change
            Attributes...

Notes

Within the DOS environment (and therefore within
Windows), files can possess properties, or
attributes, that define how they are treated by the
operating system. There are four attributes that can
be modified by this command. They are

Read-only   If the read-only attribute is enabled,
the file cannot be deleted or changed. It can only
be read by a program.

Archive   If the archive attribute is enabled, it
means that the file has been changed since it
was last backed up.

System   If the system attribute is enabled, it
means the file is designated as a file to be used
by the operating system (DOS). System files are
not normally displayed in directory listings.

Hidden   If the hidden attribute is enabled, it
means that the file will not appear in normal
directory listings—it is hidden from view.

You can still view system and hidden files by telling
Windows to display them. This is done using the
View Include command in the File Manager.

You should note that you can only change attributes
for files; you cannot change them for subdirectories.

CHANGE SYSTEM SETTINGS

Setup

The Change System Settings command lets you change your system's hardware configuration.

Menu Structure

Options | Change System Settings...

Steps

Keyboard: ALT-O-C
Shortcut: None
Mouse: Click on Options menu, then click on Change System Settings...

Notes

This command should only be used when you change the hardware attached to your computer system. With it you can change your display adapter, keyboard, mouse, and network type. When you select this command, you will see a dialog box similar to the following:

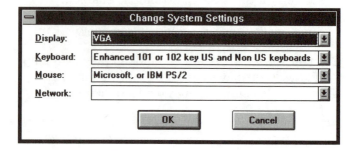

Click on the arrow to the right of the item you wish to change. You will be shown a list of available options, from which you can choose the appropriate hardware. If Windows needs to copy driver files, you may be prompted to enter the drive and path of those files. These could either be on your original Windows disks or on disks supplied by the hardware vendor.

Complete hardware setup guidance and instructions are beyond the scope of this pocket reference. For more information, see *Windows 3: The Complete Reference* by Tom Sheldon, published by Osborne/McGraw-Hill.

Tips

If you are copying Windows to a new computer, don't just copy all your program files unless the new system has the same hardware as the old system. Windows uses a series of drivers to maximize I/O hardware. If the hardware is changed and the drivers aren't (which is what happens if you copy files to a dissimilar system), then Windows will not work properly. The easiest way to work through this is to go through the Windows Setup again (a new installation) on the new system.

CLOSE ALL DIRECTORIES

File Manager

The Close All Directories command closes all the directory windows with a single command.

Menu Structure

Window | Close All Directories

Steps

Keyboard: ALT-W-A
Shortcut: None
Mouse: Click on Window menu, then click on Close All Directories

Notes

While you can close directory windows individually (see the Close Window command, next), the Close All Directories command allows you to close all of them at once.

CLOSE WINDOW

System-wide

The Close Window command closes the current window.

Menu Structure

Control | Close

Steps

Keyboard: Alt-dash-C for a document window, Alt-
Spacebar-C for all other windows
Shortcut: Ctrl-F4 for a document window, Alt-F4
for all other windows
Mouse: Click on the Control menu, then click on
Close

Notes

The Control menu is accessed through the icon in
the very upper-left corner of a window.

The Close Window command allows you to close
the current window. If the window represents an
application program, the program is terminated and
control is returned to a program in another window.

Tips

If you are using a mouse, you can close a window
very quickly by simply double-clicking on the
Control Menu icon for the window you want to
close.

COLLAPSE BRANCH

File Manager

The Collapse Branch command suppresses the
display of subdirectories within a directory.

Menu Structure

Tree | Collapse Branch

Steps

Keyboard: ALT-T-C
Shortcut: — (dash)
Mouse: Click on Tree menu, then click on
Collapse Branch

Notes

When using the directory tree in the File Manager,
the Collapse Branch command allows you to
suppress the detail about subdirectories within a
directory. A *branch* is another word for a
subdirectory. So, this command allows you to
collapse subdirectories. For example, compare the
following two screens. The first shows the
subdirectory E:\BC7 fully expanded; the second
shows the same directory after the Collapse Branch
command has been used.

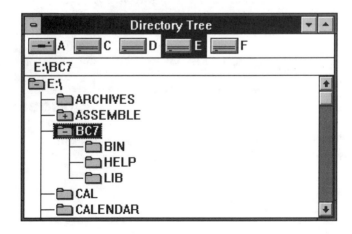

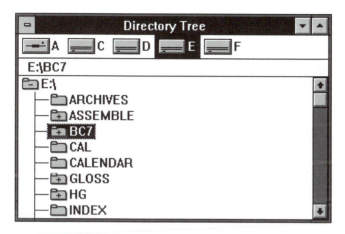

For other commands affecting the display of the
directory tree, see Expand One Level, Expand
Branch, and Expand All.

Tips

If you are using the mouse, simply click on any
subdirectory icon containing a dash, or minus sign.
This is a fast, efficient way to collapse
subdirectories.

COLOR SETTINGS

Control Panel

The Color Settings command changes the colors
used by Windows.

Menu Structure

Color

Settings | Color...

Steps

Keyboard: Alt-S-C
Shortcut: None
Mouse: Click on Settings menu, then click on
            Color...; or double-click on the Color icon

Notes

When it comes to displaying colors, Windows allows
you to completely configure how your environment
will appear. When you use this command, you are
given the option of selecting a predefined color
scheme. Windows comes with the following
schemes predefined:

Windows default	Ocean
Arizona	Patchwork
Bordeaux	Rugby
Designer	Pastel
Fluorescent	Wing tips
Monochrome	

You can define additional color schemes by clicking
on the Color Palette button. Windows allows you to
change the colors of the following screen elements:

Active border	Desktop
Active title bar	Inactive border
Application workspace	Inactive title bar

Menu bar   Window background
Menu text   Window frame
Scroll bars   Window text
Title bar text

Between sessions, Windows remembers the colors
you set. You should only have to set them once.
However, you are free to experiment and change
colors whenever you desire.

Tips

How your colors appear will depend, in large part,
on the type of video display and monitor you are
using. If you use color combinations that offer
adequate contrast on a color monitor, and you later
change to a monochrome monitor, you will be
disappointed if you find you cannot discern your
text or menus. Make sure you make color changes
to a "safe" setting before making drastic hardware
changes.

CONFIRMATION OPTIONS

File Manager

The Confirmation Options allow you to specify
when the File Manager should check with you
before taking an action.

Menu Structure

Options | Confirmation...

Steps

Keyboard: ALT–O- C
Shortcut: None
Mouse: Click on Options menu, then click on Confirmation...

Notes

This is an insurance command. Normally, the File Manager checks with you whenever it is about to do anything that could be potentially destructive. The Confirmation Options allow you to modify the amount of confirmation insurance applied to the File Manager. There are four options you can set with this command:

Confirm on Delete   If Confirm on Delete is selected, the File Manager will ask for confirmation before deleting a file. If you are deleting a large group of files, this individual confirmation can get tedious.

Confirm on Subtree Delete   If Confirm on Subtree Delete is selected, the File Manager will ask for confirmation before removing a subdirectory.

Confirm on Replace   If Confirm on Replace is selected, the File Manager will ask for confirmation before completing an operation that would overwrite the contents of an existing file.

Confirm on Mouse Operation   Some File Manager operations are very easy to do with a mouse. If Confirm on Mouse Operation is selected, you will be asked for confirmation before the File Manager completes a dragging, moving, or copying operation done with the mouse.

Tip

If you turn messaging off, be sure to turn it back on if you think you may need it in a future File Manager session.

CONNECT NET DRIVE

File Manager

The Connect Net Drive command makes a network drive accessible from Windows.

Menu Structure

Disk | Connect Net Drive...

Steps

Keyboard: Alt-D-N
Shortcut: None
Mouse: Click on Disk menu, then click on Connect Net Drive...

Notes

If you have already connected and logged onto your network before beginning Windows, chances are that all your defined network drives are already available. Within the File Manager, network drives have an icon that looks like this:

| NET |

If, however, you have not already hooked up with the network, this command allows you to define which drives should be used to access the network. You are asked to provide the drive letter (one currently not in use), along with the full network path to assign to the drive letter. Optionally, you can provide login information, if necessary.

When successfully completed, you can access the network through the drive you have set up.

COPY

Help System

The Copy command copies the current major Help System section to the Clipboard.

Menu Structure

Edit | Copy

Steps

Keyboard: Alt-E-C
Shortcut: Ctrl-Ins
Mouse: Click on Edit menu, then click on Copy

Notes

Sometimes it is helpful to see something in your own wording. If you want to rewrite a portion of the Help System, you can do so by using the Copy command. This will copy the text of the help section on your screen into the Clipboard. Then you can use the Clipboard to paste the text into another program such as a word processor.

Remember that each time you copy or delete something, whatever was in the Clipboard before is lost. It is overwritten with the information you just copied (or deleted).

Tips

If you simply want a hard copy printout of the help section, see the Print Topic command.

COPY DISKETTE

File Manager

The Copy Diskette command copies the contents of one diskette to another.

Menu Structure

Disk | Copy Diskette...

Steps

Keyboard: Alt–D–C
Shortcut: None
Mouse: Click on Disk menu, then click on Copy
         Diskette...

Notes

The Copy Diskette command allows you to make copies of entire diskettes. If you only want to copy files, see the Copy File command.

Before selecting the Copy Diskette command you must have chosen a disk drive (typically drive A or drive B) as the current drive. You can only copy diskettes of like capacity. This means that you cannot copy a 360K diskette to a 1.2MB diskette, nor can you copy from a 5.25-inch to a 3.5-inch diskette.

Warning: Copy Diskette is a destructive command. It will erase any data on the destination diskette, overwriting it with the information copied from the source diskette.

Tips

Always make backup copies of your important diskettes. The time and effort spent making copies will be repaid in full if just one of your original disks goes bad.

To copy everything between dissimilar diskette types, simply use the Copy File command with the *.* wildcard characters.

COPY FILE

File Manager

The Copy File command copies files or directories from one place to another.

Menu Structure

File | Copy...

Steps

Keyboard: ALT-F-C
Shortcut: F8
Mouse: Click on File menu, then click on Copy...

Notes

This function allows you to copy files or entire
subdirectories from one place to another. If the
place you are copying from (the *source*) and the
place you are copying to (the *destination*) are both
on the same disk, and you are using a mouse, hold
down the CTRL key and drag the icon for the file or
directory to the destination. If desired, the
destination can be the icon for another drive.

If you are not using a mouse, you should select the
Copy command. You can then specify the *from* and
to locations for the operation, using wildcard
characters to copy multiple files in one operation.
The source and destination do not need to be on the
same drive.

Tips

If you are using a mouse and the source and
destination are on different drives, you can open
multiple windows for the directories on the differing
drives. Then simply drag the files or subdirectories
between windows. There is no need to hold down
the CTRL key in this instance.

COPY PROGRAM ITEM

Program Manager

The Copy Program Item command allows you to duplicate application program icons in the Program Manager.

Menu Structure

File | Copy...

Steps

Keyboard: ALT-F-C
Shortcut: None
Mouse: Click on File menu, then click on Copy...

Notes

For readers who are not using a mouse, the Copy Program Item command is what you use to copy program icons from one program group to another. Select the icon you wish to copy, and then issue this command. You will be prompted for the name of the group to which you want the program copied.

Tips

If you are using a mouse, you can accomplish this task much more easily. All you need to do is hold down the CTRL key and drag the program icon to the program group where you want it copied.

Use the Move command if you want to move an icon into another program group.

CREATE DIRECTORY

File Manager

The Create Directory command allows you to create subdirectories.

Menu Structure

File | Create Directory...

Steps

Keyboard: Alt-F-E
Shortcut: None
Mouse: Click on File menu, then click on Create Directory...

Notes

This command allows you to create a directory, into which you can then place files. When you choose this command, you are asked to provide the name of the directory you wish to create. You can either type a single name (in which case the subdirectory will be created in the current directory), or you can provide a full path name of the subdirectory to be created.

DATE & TIME SETTINGS

Control Panel

The Date & Time Settings command changes the
date and time used by the system.

Menu Structure

Date/Time

Settings | Date/Time...

Steps

Keyboard: ALT-S-T
Shortcut: None
Mouse: Click on Settings menu, then click on
              Date/Time...; or double-click on the
              Date/Time icon

Notes

Internally, your computer system keeps track of the
time and date. Windows accesses this information
in order to control some functions. For instance, the
Appointment accessory uses the date and time
information to operate properly.

This command allows you to change both the date
and time. You can either type in new information,
or use the up and down control buttons to change it.

Tips

The format used to display the date and time is
controlled by the International Settings command.
See that command for more information.

DEFINE BOOKMARK

Help System

The Define Bookmark command places a marker at a
commonly referenced point in the Help System.

Menu Structure

Bookmark | Define...

Steps

Keyboard: Alt-M-D
Shortcut: None
Mouse: Click on Bookmark menu, then click on
Define...

Notes

Just as bookmarks help you mark your place in
books made of paper, so do electronic bookmarks
make it easier for you to locate your place in the
Help System. The Define Bookmark command
allows you to place bookmarks anywhere you like
within a Help System volume. The name you give
the bookmark is up to you; after the bookmark is
added, the name will appear in the Bookmark menu.

A bookmark does more than just mark a help topic. It actually saves your screen location. When you later return to a place marked by a bookmark, the screen will appear exactly the same way it appeared when you placed the bookmark.

Tips

This command is also used to delete a bookmark. To do this, select the Define Bookmark command. When the menu appears, click on the bookmark you want to delete, and then click the Delete button.

DELETE

File Manager

The Delete command under the File Manager allows deletion of files or subdirectories.

Menu Structure

File | Delete...

Steps

Keyboard: Alt-F-D
Shortcut: Del
Mouse: Click on File menu, then click on
            Delete...

Notes

This command allows you to delete files or subdirectories. If a file has the read-only attribute enabled, it cannot be deleted without first disabling the attribute. For more information on attributes, see the Change Attribute command.

When you choose the Delete command, you are presented with a dialog box that asks you to specify the file or directory you wish to delete. The default is the currently selected file or directory. If the default is not correct, you can type in another file or directory specification.

When you delete the item, you are asked to confirm your intentions. If you select Yes, the file and/or subdirectory are erased from the disk. Note that confirmation only occurs if you have not disabled the Confirm on Delete and Confirm on Subtree Delete options. See the Confirmation Options command for more information.

Warning: Delete is a destructive command. It will erase any file or subdirectory you specify, so use it with care. Be sure you really want to delete something before you use this command.

You can delete a program using this command and still find that the program icon used by the Program Manager was not deleted. You need to use the Delete command under the Program Manager to delete the icon, as explained next.

DELETE

Program Manager

The Delete command under the Program Manager allows deletion of a program group or an application program.

Menu Structure

File | Delete...

Steps

Keyboard: ALT-F-D
Shortcut: DEL
Mouse: Click on File menu, then click on Delete...

Notes

Before you select this command, make sure you have selected the program group or application program you wish to delete. Regardless of which type of item you are deleting, you will be asked to confirm your choice. If you continue, then the program or program group is deleted. Once deleted, it is no longer available from the Program Manager.

Typically you will not need to use this command. It is provided for advanced users of Windows, and is beyond the scope of this pocket reference. For more information, see *Windows 3: The Complete Reference* by Tom Sheldon.

DELETE CLIPBOARD

Clipboard

The Delete Clipboard command deletes the contents of the Clipboard.

Menu Structure

Edit | Delete

Steps

Keyboard: Alt-E-D
Shortcut: Del
Mouse: Click on Edit menu, then click on Delete

Notes

This command is used to clear the Clipboard. After completion, whatever was in the Clipboard is lost, and there is no way to recover it (unless you have previously saved it to a Clipboard file). The destructive nature of this command is why Windows asks you to confirm your actions.

Warning: Delete Clipboard is a destructive command. It will erase the contents of the Clipboard permanently, so use it with care. Be sure you really want to delete the selected item before using this command.

DESELECT ALL

File Manager

The Deselect All command disassembles the file selection group you have created.

Menu Structure

File | Deselect All

Steps

Keyboard: ALT-F-L
Shortcut: CTRL-\
Mouse: Click on File menu, then click on Deselect All

Notes

The Deselect All command is only available when a directory window is open and selected; it is not available from the directory tree. When you use the command, all of the files in the current selection group are deselected, and the file cursor is left on the first file in the window.

Also see the Select All command.

DESKTOP SETTINGS

Control Panel

The Desktop Settings command changes the
appearance of your desktop, including patterns and
wallpaper, cursor appearance, and icon spacing.

Menu Structure

Desktop

Settings I Desktop...

Steps

Keyboard: Alt-S-D
Shortcut: None
Mouse: Click on Settings menu, then click on
Desktop...; or double-click on the
Desktop icon

Notes

This command controls the setting of several facets
of your desktop. These include:

Pattern   Pattern refers to the design used to
cover the desktop. The colors used to display the
pattern are controlled by the Color Settings
command.

Wallpaper   Wallpaper refers to the picture used to overlay the desktop pattern. A graphics file saved in a special bit-map format (these have a BMP file extension) can be used for the wallpaper. BMP files can be created with programs such as the Paintbrush accessory. Display options include centering the picture on the desktop, or repeating an image as many times as necessary to fill the desktop with a pattern instead of a solid color (*tiling*).

Cursor Blink Rate   The cursor blink rate is the speed at which the cursor blinks while awaiting user input.

Icons   This Icons option determines spacing—how close (in pixels) icons are placed in relation to each other within a window. This value is used by Windows when aligning icons within a window.

Sizing Grid   The two settings here control the *granularity* and *border width* used by Windows. The value you set for granularity is used by Windows to establish a grid for aligning icons within a window. Windows multiplies this granularity value by 8 to determine how many pixels apart the invisible grid lines should be. The border width setting specifies how many pixels wide the border is around individual windows.

There are several stock patterns and wallpaper files you may wish to use; these come with Windows. You can also find additional wallpaper graphics from users groups or from bulletin board systems such as CompuServe.

DISCONNECT NET DRIVE

File Manager

The Disconnect Net Drive command breaks a drive's
link with a network.

Menu Structure

Disk | Disconnect Net Drive...

Steps

Keyboard: Alt-D-D
Shortcut: None
Mouse: Click on Disk menu, then click on
Disconnect Net Drive...

Notes

Chances are you will never have to use this
command. But if, for some reason, you need to
disable a drive's mapping to a network drive, this is
the command to do it.

When you choose this command, all you need to do
is provide the drive letter of the drive you want to
disconnect. This must be a network drive
recognized by Windows. You can tell which drives
are recognized by Windows as network drives by
looking at the icon representing the drive. A
network drive has an icon that looks like this:

Choose the command, supply the drive letter, confirm your choice, and the network drive is disconnected.

EXIT WINDOWS

Program Manager

The Exit Windows command has you leave the Windows environment and return to DOS.

Menu Structure

File | Exit Windows...

Steps

Keyboard: ALT-F-X
Shortcut: None
Mouse: Click on Files menu, then click on Exit Windows...

Notes

When you are finished with Windows, you can exit to DOS by selecting this command. Make sure you really want to leave, as any programs running in the background will be canceled, and any print jobs in the Print Manager will be lost.

When you choose to exit, Windows will prompt you to make sure this is what you really want to do. If you want any system changes you have made (including moving icons and resizing windows) to be saved until the next Windows session, you

should make sure the Save Changes option is
selected.

Tips

If you are using a mouse, to exit Windows you can
double-click on the Control Menu icon for the
Program Manager.

EXPAND ALL

File Manager

The Expand All command displays every
subdirectory for the current drive.

Menu Structure

Tree | Expand All

Steps

Keyboard: ALT-T-A
Shortcut: CTRL-*
Mouse: Click on Tree menu, then click on
            Expand All

Notes

When using the directory tree in the File Manager,
this command allows you to see every subdirectory
on a drive. It is the same as moving the directory
tree cursor to the root directory level and using the
Expand Branch command. All subdirectories are
displayed, down to the lowest level.

For other commands affecting the display of the
directory tree, see Collapse Branch, Expand Branch,
and Expand One Level.

EXPAND BRANCH

File Manager

The Expand Branch command displays any
subdirectories within the selected directory, down
to the lowest level.

Menu Structure

Tree | Expand Branch

Steps

Keyboard: Alt-T-B
Shortcut: *
Mouse: Click on Tree menu, then click on
Expand Branch

Notes

When using the directory tree in the File Manager,
this command allows you to see all subdirectories
within a directory. It is similar to the Expand One
Level command, but Expand Branch will expand
multiple levels of directories, starting at the selected
directory.

For screens showing example directory trees that
are expanded and collapsed, see the Collapse
Branch command. For other commands affecting

the display of the directory tree, see also the Expand All and Expand One Level commands.

EXPAND ONE LEVEL

File Manager

The Expand One Level command displays any subdirectories within the selected directory.

Menu Structure

Tree | Expand One Level

Steps

Keyboard: ALT-T-X
Shortcut: +
Mouse: Click on Tree menu, then click on Expand One Level

Notes

When using the directory tree in the File Manager, this command allows you to see detail about what subdirectories are within a directory. For screens showing example directory trees that are expanded and collapsed, see the Collapse Branch command.

For other commands affecting the display of the directory tree, see also Expand Branch and Expand All.

Tips

If you are using the mouse, simply click on any subdirectory icon containing a plus sign. This is a fast, efficient way to expand subdirectories.

FLASH IF INACTIVE

Print Manager

If the Print Manager is inactive, the Flash if Inactive command causes the Print Manager icon or title bar to blink if an error in printing is detected.

Menu Structure

Options | Flash if Inactive

Steps

Keyboard: Alt-O-F
Shortcut: None
Mouse: Click on Options menu, then click on Flash if Inactive

Notes

The Print Manager governs how Windows interacts with your printer. It is a spooling utility, and its use is completely optional. Since printers are usually slower than computers, a spooling utility (such as the Print Manager) allows information to be sent to your printer at the speed your printer can accept it, freeing up your computer to work on other tasks.

This is a toggle option, meaning that the same command turns the option on and off. When you select the command the first time, the error notification status for the Print Manager is changed, and a check mark appears beside the command on the menu. If you use another error notification command (Alert Always or Ignore if Inactive), the check mark moves to the other command setting.

Typically the work done by the Print Manager is not done in an active window. It is usually done in the background while you are concentrating on other, more pressing tasks. Using this command determines how the Print Manager notifies you if it detects a condition that demands your attention.

After this command, if the Print Manager is in an inactive window or if it is minimized, the following will happen when an error is detected:

1. The title bar at the top of the Print Manager window will flash. (Obviously, this does not happen if the Print Manager is minimized.)

2. The icon for the Print Manager will blink.

When you make the Print Manager the active window, the error message dialog box will be displayed. This is the default setting for Print Manager error notification.

If the Print Manager is already the active window, then the error message dialog box is displayed immediately.

FONT SETTINGS

Control Panel

The Font Settings command allows viewing,
adding, and removing system font sets.

Menu Structure

Fonts

Settings | Fonts...

Steps

Keyboard: Alt-S-F
Shortcut: None
Mouse: Click on Settings menu, then click on
Fonts...; or double-click on the Fonts
icon

Notes

Windows supports a multitude of screen and printer
fonts. It comes with a sizeable collection of fonts
that can be used in Windows applications (such as
the Write accessory). This command allows you to
view representative samples of the screen fonts, as
well as add new fonts and remove fonts that were
previously added.

If you choose to add fonts, you will have the
opportunity to select a font file to add. This will
probably be a file provided by a third party. You
should specify where the font resides, select the

font file, and then click on OK. When you do, Windows adds the font to the available font list.

When you remove a font, it is not deleted from your hard drive. It is only removed from the list of fonts actively available to Windows. You may wish to remove fonts that you rarely or never use. Doing so will free some memory and hard disk space for other uses.

Tips

Keep in mind that working with fonts requires both memory and processing time. If you use a lot of fonts, chances are good that your overall processing time will be longer for any given task. On the other hand, judicious use of fonts can give your work a very attractive professional appearance.

Never remove the Helvetica font, since it is used by Windows for window titles and dialog boxes.

FORMAT DISKETTE

File Manager

The Format Diskette command prepares a blank diskette to receive files.

Menu Structure

Disk | Format Diskette...

Steps

Keyboard: Alt-D-F
Shortcut: None
Mouse: Click on Disk menu, then click on Format Disk...

Notes

Before you can store information on a diskette, it must be formatted. This command allows you to format a diskette and optionally put system files on it. These system files are necessary if you want to be able to make the diskette bootable.

When you choose this command, you are given the opportunity to select which disk drive to use. (If you do not physically have a B drive, Windows assumes you will format using drive A.) Select a drive. You will then be able to indicate whether the diskette is to be high capacity, and whether this is meant to be a system disk. Make your choices and select OK; the diskette will be formatted.

 Warning: Format Diskette is a destructive command. It will erase any existing data on a diskette. Be sure you really want to format a diskette before you use this command.

Tips

If you have already formatted a diskette, and you later decide you need to make it a system diskette, you do not have to reformat it. Use the Make System Diskette command; it is quicker and easier.

HIGH PRIORITY

Print Manager

The High Priority command sets the priority level
for printing jobs handled by the Print Manager.

Menu Structure

Options | High Priority

Steps

Keyboard: Alt-O-H
Shortcut: None
Mouse: Click on Options menu, then click on
High Priority

Notes

The Print Manager governs how Windows interacts
with your printer. It is a spooling utility, and its use
is completely optional. Since printers are usually
slower than computers, a spooling utility (such as
the Print Manager) allows information to be sent to
your printer at the speed your printer can accept it,
freeing up your computer to work on other tasks.

This is a toggle option, meaning that the same
command turns the option on and off. When you
select the command the first time, the priority level
for what the Print Manager does is set at its highest
level, and a check mark appears beside the
command on the menu. If you use another priority
command (Low Priority or Medium Priority), the
check mark moves to the other priority level.

This command controls what relative percentage of your computer's time is spent processing printing jobs. When set to high priority, then the work done by the Print Manager takes the largest percentage of your computer's time, even when there are other tasks running. It also means that your other tasks take longer to complete than if you used a lower priority setting for the Print Manager.

This command only affects system operation if there are print jobs waiting to print.

Tips

If you find that your other tasks are of greater importance than what you are printing out, use a lower priority setting for the Print Manager.

If you find that it is imperative that your other tasks not be interrupted by what the Print Manager is doing, pause output to the printers by selecting the printer and clicking on the Pause button.

IGNORE IF INACTIVE

Print Manager

The Ignore if Inactive command turns off Print Manager error reporting when the Print Manager is inactive.

Menu Structure

Options | Ignore if Inactive

Steps

Keyboard: ALT-O-I
Shortcut: None
Mouse: Click on Options menu, then click on
Ignore if Inactive

Notes

The Print Manager governs how Windows interacts
with your printer. It is a spooling utility, and its use
is completely optional. Since printers are usually
slower than computers, a spooling utility (such as
the Print Manager) allows information to be sent to
your printer at the speed your printer can accept it,
freeing up your computer to work on other tasks.

This is a toggle option, meaning the same command
turns the option on and off. When you select the
command the first time, the error notification status
for the Print Manager is changed, and a check mark
appears beside the command on the menu. If you
use another error notification command (Alert
Always or Flash if Inactive), the check mark moves
to the other command setting.

Typically the work done by the Print Manager is not
done in an active window. It is usually done in the
background while you are concentrating on other,
more pressing tasks. Using this command
determines how the Print Manager notifies you if it
detects a condition that demands your attention.

After this command, if the Print Manager is in an
inactive window or is minimized, then any condition
requiring your attention is ignored. If the Print
Manager is the active window, however, the error
message dialog box is displayed immediately.

Tip

It is best not to use this notification option. If you do, you run the risk of not getting some of your printed output because you were not able to correct a situation that required your intervention.

INDEX

Help System

Index is the button in the Help System that automatically jumps to and displays the index for the current Help System file.

Menu Structure

Steps

Keyboard: ALT-I
Shortcut: None
Mouse: Click on Index button

Notes

The Help System built into Windows is very powerful. It displays information from a help file in a consistent and clear manner. These help files have the HLP file extension. If, when loading an application program, Windows discovers that there is a help file that has the same root filename as the application program, that help file is opened and ready for use.

This command displays the index for the help file currently loaded. The depth and adequacy of the index is up to whomever designed the help file. The Index button is available all the time, even when the index is currently being displayed.

If there is more than one index for the help file, this command displays the first index in the file.

Tips

The F1 key is the universal help key. When you press it, the Help System is started and the index is displayed. This is the same as opening the Help System from the menu and pressing the Index button.

INTERNATIONAL SETTINGS

Control Panel

The International Settings command allows you to change global values for language, keyboard, measurements, date, time, and numbers.

Menu Structure

International

Settings | International...

Steps

Keyboard: Alt-S-I
Shortcut: None
Mouse: Click on Settings menu, then click on
             International...; or double-click on the
             International icon

Notes

Use of computers, and thus use of Windows, is not
solely limited to the United States. This command
allows you to change settings to customize
Windows and Windows applications for differing
international display standards.

You can change the following with this command:

Country   Allows you to select a desired country
from a list presented onscreen. When a country
is selected, default options are set for that
country. You can alter the individual settings for
that country, however, by changing any of the
other options listed in this rest of this section.

Language   The Language setting is used to
change the sorting and case conversion
procedures of some Windows applications.

Keyboard Layout   If you use an international
keyboard (one for a country other than the United
States), select the appropriate country from the
list. Your selection informs Windows how to
interpret what you type.

Measurement   The Measurement setting lets
you select English or Metric measurements.

List Separator   The List Separator setting determines which character is used to distinguish between elements in a list of words. Typically this is the comma, but it can be changed to any character you desire.

Date Format   The Date Format setting lets you choose how you want Windows to display dates.

Time Format   The Time Format setting lets you choose how you want Windows to display the time of day.

Currency Format   With the Currency Format setting, you specify the currency symbol (the dollar sign, the British pound sign, and so on) and its placement in relation to numbers, how negative numbers are represented, and how many decimal places to use.

Number Format   With the Number Format setting, you select which characters to use to separate thousands and to signify decimal values, as well as whether leading zeros are displayed.

Tips

Use of the International Settings command is not just for international users. You may wish to change settings because of a personal preference for how the time and date are displayed.

KEYBOARD SETTINGS

Control Panel

The Keyboard Settings command changes the repeat rate for the keyboard.

Menu Structure

Keyboard

Settings | Keyboard...

Steps

Keyboard: Alt-S-K
Shortcut: None
Mouse: Click on Settings menu, then click on Keyboard...; or double-click on the Keyboard icon

Notes

The Keyboard Settings only allow you to change the rate at which keypresses repeat when you hold down a key. This is a relative setting, on a scale of slow to fast. You should select a setting based on your typing ability and preferences. The slower the setting, the longer you will need to hold a key before it repeats.

This command does not allow you to change the type of keyboard you are using. You should see the Change System Settings command for more information on doing that.

LABEL DISK

File Manager

The Label Disk command allows you to set, change, or delete a label assigned to a disk.

Menu Structure

Disk | Label Disk...

Steps

Keyboard: ALT-D-L
Shortcut: None
Mouse: Click on Disk menu, then click on Label Disk...

Notes

Assigning a label to a disk is really nothing more than naming the disk. This name can be up to 11 characters long, and should follow the same naming conventions used for naming disk files.

When you select this command, you will be shown any existing disk label. If you want to delete an existing disk label, simply press the BACKSPACE key once right after selecting this command.

LOW PRIORITY

Print Manager

The Low Priority command sets the priority level for printing jobs handled by the Print Manager.

Menu Structure

Options | Low Priority

Steps

Keyboard: ALT-O-P
Shortcut: None
Mouse: Click on Options menu, then click on Low Priority

Notes

The Print Manager governs how Windows interacts with your printer. It is a spooling utility, and its use is completely optional. Since printers are usually slower than computers, a spooling utility (such as the Print Manager) allows information to be sent to your printer at the speed your printer can accept it, freeing up your computer to work on other tasks.

This is a toggle option, meaning that the same command turns the option on and off. When you select the command the first time, the priority level for what Print Manager does is set at the lowest level, and a check mark appears beside the command on the menu. If you use another priority command (Medium Priority or High Priority), the check mark moves to the other priority level.

The Low Priority command controls what relative percentage of your computer's time is spent processing printing jobs. When set to low priority, then the work done by the Print Manager takes a lesser percentage when your computer is busy doing other tasks. It also means that your other tasks receive a greater percentage of time, and therefore complete faster.

This command only affects system operation if there are print jobs waiting to print. Also, the throughput of the Print Manager is affected by this command only if there are other demands on your computer's time (there are other active tasks running).

Tips

If you find that your print jobs are not completing fast enough, or you are getting time-out errors on your printer, select a higher priority setting for the Print Manager.

LOWER CASE

File Manager

The Lower Case command instructs the File Manager to use lowercase characters when displaying directory and file information.

Menu Structure

Options | Lower Case

Steps

Keyboard: Alt-O-L
Shortcut: None
Mouse: Click on Options menu, then click on Lower Case

Notes

This is a toggle option, meaning that the same command turns the option on and off. When you select the command the first time, the display is changed to lower case and a check mark appears beside the command on the menu. Select Lower Case again, and the check mark disappears.

If Lower Case is enabled, Windows automatically converts file and directory displays to lowercase. This does not affect menus or other Windows operations; it only affects the display of file and directory names.

The use of this command is a personal preference. It does not affect the overall functioning of Windows.

MAKE SYSTEM DISKETTE

File Manager

The Make System Diskette command transfers system files to a formatted diskette.

Menu Structure

Disk | Make System Diskette...

Steps

Keyboard: Alt-D-M
Shortcut: None
Mouse: Click on Disk menu, then click on Make
             System Diskette...

Notes

If you want to make a diskette bootable, you must
first transfer system files to it. The Make System
Diskette command accomplishes that task with a
previously formatted diskette.

In order for this command to work, you must have
the current drive set to the one from which you
normally boot your computer. For most people, this
will be drive C. If you do not do this, Windows will
not be able to locate the system files and will
display an error message.

Under certain circumstances, Windows will not be
able to complete this command. Generally this
happens if the diskette you want to make into a
system diskette already has files stored on it. You
have the greatest chance of success when you use
an empty diskette for this operation.

Tips

If the diskette is completely blank, or if you wish to
permanently erase all the files on the diskette, use
the Format Diskette command. Make sure you
select the option to make the newly formatted
diskette a system disk.

MAXIMIZE WINDOW

System-wide

The Maximize Window command expands the current window to fill the entire screen.

Menu Structure

Control | Maximize

Steps

Keyboard: ALT-DASH-X for a document window, ALT-SPACEBAR-X for all other windows
Shortcut: None
Mouse: Click on the Control menu, then click on Maximize

Notes

The Control menu is accessed through the icon in the upper-left corner of a window.

For readers who are not using a mouse, this is the command provided to expand an icon to full screen, or to expand an open window to fill the entire screen. This command is only available if the window has not already been maximized.

Tips

If you are using a mouse, simply click on the upward-pointing arrow in the upper-right corner of the screen. This does the same task as the Maximize Window command.

MEDIUM PRIORITY

Print Manager

The Medium Priority command sets the priority level for printing jobs handled by the Print Manager.

Menu Structure

Options | Medium Priority

Steps

Keyboard: ALT-O-M
Shortcut: None
Mouse: Click on Options menu, then click on Medium Priority

Notes

The Print Manager governs how Windows interacts with your printer. It is a spooling utility, and its use is completely optional. Since printers are usually slower than computers, a spooling utility (such as the Print Manager) allows information to be sent to your printer at the speed your printer can accept it, freeing up your computer to work on other tasks.

This is a toggle option, meaning that the same command turns the option on and off. When you select the command the first time, the priority level for what the Print Manager does is set at an intermediate level, and a check mark appears beside the command on the menu. If you use another priority command (Low Priority or High

Priority), the check mark moves to the other priority level.

This command controls what relative percentage of your computer's time is spent processing printing jobs. When set to medium priority, the work done by the Print Manager takes an intermediate percentage when your computer is busy doing other tasks. It also means that your other tasks take longer to complete than if you used a low priority setting for the Print Manager.

This command only affects system operation if there are print jobs waiting to print. Also, the throughput of the Print Manager is affected by this command only if there are other demands on your computer's time (there are other active tasks running).

Tips

If you find that your print jobs are not completing fast enough, or you are getting time-out errors on your printer, use the High Priority command to select a higher priority level for the Print Manager.

If you find that your other tasks are of greater importance than what you are printing out, use the Low Priority command.

If you find that it is imperative that your other tasks not be interrupted by what the Print Manager is doing, pause output to the printers by selecting the printer and clicking on the Pause button.

MINIMIZE ON USE

Program Manager or File Manager

The Minimize on Use command controls whether
the Program Manager or File Manager is
automatically minimized to a single icon when an
application is started.

Menu Structure

Options | Minimize on Use

Steps

Keyboard: Alt-O-M
Shortcut: None
Mouse: Click on Options menu, then click on
Minimize on Use

Notes

This is a toggle option, meaning that the same
command turns the option on and off. When you
select the command the first time, a check mark
appears beside the command on the menu. Select
Minimize on Use again, and the check mark
disappears.

With Minimize on Use enabled, Windows
automatically shrinks, or *minimizes*, the window
when an application is run. For instance, if you are
using the Program Manager and then start another
application without closing the Program Manager
first, the Program Manager is minimized to an icon.
The same is true when running applications from

within the File Manager. The screen is then maximized for the application being run.

When you exit the application program, you will need to open the Program Manager or File Manager icon again. The benefit of this command is that it automatically causes maximum screen space to be given to the application on which you're working.

The use of this command is a personal preference. It does not affect the overall functioning of Windows.

MINIMIZE WINDOW

System-wide

The Minimize Window command shrinks the current window to an icon.

Menu Structure

Control | Minimize

Steps

Keyboard: ALT-DASH-N for a document window, ALT-SPACEBAR-N for all other windows

Shortcut: None

Mouse: Click on the Control menu, then click on Minimize

Notes

The Control menu is accessed through the icon in the upper-left corner of a window.

For readers who are not using a mouse, this is the command provided to shrink a window to a single icon. This command is only available if the window has not already been minimized.

Tips

If you are using a mouse, simply click on the downward-pointing arrow in the upper-right corner of the screen. This does the same task as the Minimize Window command.

MOUSE SETTINGS

Control Panel

The Mouse Settings command lets you change how your mouse functions in relation to Windows.

Menu Structure

Mouse

Settings I Mouse...

Steps

Keyboard: ALT-S-M
Shortcut: None
Mouse: Click on Settings menu, then click on Mouse...; or double-click on the Mouse icon

Notes

If you are like most Windows users, your mouse is integral to productive use of Windows. This command allows you to change several settings that affect how Windows reacts to your mouse. These settings are

Mouse Tracking Speed   The Mouse Tracking Speed setting controls how fast the mouse curser onscreen moves when you move the mouse. This is a relative setting, from slow to fast; the slower the setting, the slower the mouse cursor moves.

Double Click Speed   The Double Click Speed setting controls the amount of time allowed between mouse clicks before the two clicks can be considered one double-click. This is a relative setting, from slow to fast; the slower the setting, the more time allowed between successive clicks.

Swap Left/Right Buttons   Toggle the Swap Left/Right Buttons setting if you wish the actions caused by the left and right mouse buttons to be reversed.

MOVE

Program Manager

The Move command allows you to move a program from one program group to another.

Menu Structure

File | Move...

Steps

Keyboard: Alt-F-M
Shortcut: None
Mouse: Click on File menu, then click on Move...

Notes

For readers who are not using a mouse, the Move command is what you use to move program icons from one program group to another. Select the icon you wish to move, and then issue this command. You will be prompted for the name of the group to which you want the program moved.

Tips

If you are using a mouse, you can accomplish this task much more easily. All you need to do is click on the program icon and drag it to the program group where you want it to be.

Use the Copy Program Item command if you want to duplicate an icon into another program group.

MOVE FILE

File Manager

The Move File command moves files or directories from one place to another.

Menu Structure

File | Move...

Steps

Keyboard: Alt-F-M
Shortcut: F7
Mouse: Click on File menu, then click on Move...

Notes

The Move File command allows you to move files or
entire subdirectories from one place to another. If
the place you are moving from (the *source*) and the
place you are moving to (the *destination*) are both
on the same disk, and you are using a mouse, you
simply need to drag the icon for the file or directory
to the destination. If desired, the destination can be
the icon for another drive.

If you are not using a mouse, you should select the
Move File command. You can then specify the *from*
and *to* locations for the move, using wildcard
characters to move multiple files in one operation.
The source and destination do not need to be on the
same drive.

Basically, Move File copies the designated files or
subdirectories to the new location then deletes
them from their original location. Note that if you
are moving subdirectories on the same drive, you
will be asked if you want to remove the original
subtree (subdirectory and associated files). If the
source and destination are on different drives, you
are not given this option unless you hold down the
Alt key while dragging the icon.

Tips

If you are using a mouse and the source and destination are on different drives, you can open multiple windows for the directories on the differing drives. Then simply drag the files or subdirectories between windows.

MOVE WINDOW

System-wide

The Move Window command allows you to move a window around the screen.

Menu Structure

Control | Move

Steps

Keyboard: Alt-Dash-M for a document window, Alt-Spacebar-M for all other windows
Shortcut: None
Mouse: Click on the Control menu, then click on Move

Notes

The Control menu is accessed through the icon in the upper-left corner of a window.

For readers not using a mouse, the Move Window command is what you use to move individual windows around the desktop. When you select this command, a positioning cursor will appear on the screen. You can then use the arrow keys to move the window. When you are satisfied with the new window position, press ENTER to accept the new position, or ESC to cancel the move.

The use of this command is personal preference. There is no real benefit to where windows are located on the screen, other than to make your work easier.

Tips

If you have a mouse, simply click on the window's title bar and drag it to any position on the screen.

NETWORK OPTIONS

Print Manager

The Network Options let you set how the Print Manager interacts with a network.

Menu Structure

Options | Network...

Steps

Keyboard: ALT-O-N
Shortcut: None
Mouse: Click on Options menu, then click on Network...

Notes

This command is available only if you are connected
to a network, and are using printing facilities for
that network.

If you are concerned about heavy network traffic, or
if you don't want to have the Print Manager
network displays constantly updated, use this
command. When you do, you are presented with a
dialog box that allows you to change whether the
network display is updated and whether Print
Manager should print network jobs directly. Select
whichever settings you want, and click on the OK
button.

If you turn off Network Display Updating, then none
of the Print Manager network displays will be
updated until you either turn this option back on or
unless you use the Update Net Queues command.

NETWORK SETTINGS

Control Panel

The Network Settings command provides a way to
access network utilities.

Menu Structure

Network

Settings | Network...

Steps

Keyboard: Alt-S-N
Shortcut: None
Mouse: Click on Settings menu, then click on
Network...; or double-click on the
Network icon

Notes

This command is available only if your computer is
attached to a network. It provides a way for you to
access basic network utilities. When you choose
this command, you are presented with a dialog box
that indicates the type of network you are attached
to, and asks you what network utility you want to
run.

You can run any network utility; a few of them are
built into the network driver you installed with
Windows. Exactly what options are available
depends on your network. For instance, if you are
using Novell NetWare, the built-in utilities are:

Attach a File Server
Detach a File Server
Disable Broadcast Messages
Enable Broadcast Messages

For additional information about networks, see the
Connect Net Drive and Disconnect Net Drive
commands.

Tips

Make sure the communications settings used in
Windows match the communications parameters

expected by the external device. If they don't, you won't be able to establish a working connection.

NEW

Program Manager

The New command lets you designate a new program or create a new program group.

Menu Structure

File | New...

Steps

Keyboard: Alt-F-N
Shortcut: None
Mouse: Click on File menu, then click on New...

Notes

This command is most often used to add program groups to the Program Manager, but can also be used to add application programs within program groups.

When you choose this command you are asked to specify whether you are setting up a program group or a *program item*. A program item is represented in the Program Manager as an icon, and is used to start an application program. Make your choice and press Enter.

If you are adding a program group, you are asked for the description and group filename. The description is the name that appears under the icon or in the title bar when the program group is opened as a window. The group filename is the DOS file used by Windows to track what is included in this program group. You do not need to provide a group filename—Windows will create one automatically.

If you are adding a program item, you are asked for the description and the command line to be executed when the icon is selected. The description is the name that appears under the icon on the desktop, as well as in the title bar of the window when the application is running. The command line is the DOS command executed when the icon is selected, or started. This command line consists of the full path name to the program file, including the disk drive (if necessary). When you supply these items and press Enter, Windows will create an appropriate icon for the type of program you added.

If you want to change either a program group or a program item, use the Properties command.

Tips

For frequently used programs, you can have program groups created automatically by the Set Up Applications command.

If you are adding a program group, and you do not designate a filename, Windows will use the first eight legal characters of the description as a root filename, along with the extension GRP. If you have multiple groups where the first eight characters of the description are the same, you must provide a unique program group filename when creating the program group.

NEXT WINDOW

System-wide

The Next Window command makes the next
document window the active window.

Menu Structure

Control | Next

Steps

Keyboard: ALT-DASH-T
Shortcut: CTRL-F6
Mouse: Click on the Control menu, then click on
Next

Notes

The Control menu is accessed through the icon in
the upper-left corner of a window.

This command is only available if there are multiple
document windows open on your screen. This
command causes Windows to cycle through each of
them, one after the other. It is mainly provided for
users who are not using a mouse, or is useful to
access windows completely hidden by other
windows.

Tip

If you are using a mouse, and you can see any
portion of the desired window, click on that portion

to access the window. This is much faster than using the Next Window command.

OPEN

Program Manager or File Manager

The Open command lets you open a subdirectory or a file, or start a program.

Menu Structure

File | Open

Steps

Keyboard: ALT-F-O
Shortcut: ENTER
Mouse: Click on File menu, then click on Open

Notes

Within the Program Manager, the Open command is used to start applications. When you issue the Open command, Windows will attempt to load and run the currently selected application.

Within the File Manager, this command is generally used to open directories, although it can be used to open documents that are associated with programs. If you try to open a file that has no program association, you will get an error message. For more information, see the Associate File command.

When you use this command to open a directory in the File Manager, a new window for that directory is opened unless you first used the Replace on Open command.

If you use this command to open an application program or PIF file, Windows will attempt to run the application or the program associated with the PIF file.

Tips

You can also open directories or files by double-clicking on their icon.

OPEN CLIPBOARD FILE

Clipboard

The Open Clipboard File command opens and loads a previously saved Clipboard.

Menu Structure

File | Open...

Steps

Keyboard: Alt–F–O
Shortcut: None
Mouse: Click on File menu, then click on Open...

Notes

This command allows you to open Clipboard files created by the Save As command. Clipboard files have the extension CLP. The information in these files can be text or graphics; indeed, it can be any data that might be exchanged between applications via the Clipboard.

Information is put into and taken out of the Clipboard with editing commands, the most common of which are Copy, Cut, and Paste.

When you choose the Open Clipboard File command, you are prompted for a filename. You are shown a series of files with the CLP extension. You may choose one of those or directly enter a filename to be opened.

Also see the Save As command.

Tips

If you find yourself pasting the same graphic (such as a logo or special symbol) again and again, copy it into the Clipboard and save it to disk. Then you can access the file at a later date and paste it into whatever you are working on at the time.

If you use this command while there is data in the Clipboard, the old data will be cleared before the new file is loaded. If the Clipboard currently contains information you want to save, do so before using the Open Clipboard File command.

OPEN FILE

Help System

The Open File command opens a specific Help System file.

Menu Structure

File | Open...

Steps

Keyboard: Alt–F–O
Shortcut: None
Mouse: Click on File menu, then click on Open...

Notes

The information displayed by the Windows Help
System is contained in a series of help files. When
you enter the Help System, Windows displays the
help file that it deems most appropriate to the
context of what you are doing. This command
allows you to open a different help file from the one
Windows would show you.

Help files have the file extension HLP. When you
choose the Open File command, you are shown a
list of all the help files available in the current
directory. You can navigate to another drive or
directory to search for more help files, if desired.
When you have found the help file you want to use,
select it and click on the Open button. The help file
is loaded and displayed.

Tips

Use this command if you want to refer to help for a
particular program, but don't want to go through
the hassle of loading the program and then
accessing the Help System.

OTHER NET QUEUE

Print Manager

The Other Net Queue command lets you view the status of network printer queues to which you are not currently connected.

Menu Structure

View | Other Net Queue...

Steps

Keyboard: Alt-V-O
Shortcut: None
Mouse: Click on View menu, then click on Other Net Queue...

Notes

The Other Net Queue command is available only if you are connected to a network and using printing facilities for that network.

This command allows you to view the print jobs waiting in other network print queues besides the ones you are connected to. In this way, you can determine if you want to print to one of the other queues. If you do, you will still need to connect to that queue using the Printer Settings command from the Control Panel.

A network print queue is different than the print queue maintained by the Print Manager. The Print Manager maintains a queue of print jobs for your

computer alone. A network print queue is for the
print jobs of all users attached to the network.

PORT SETTINGS

Control Panel

The Port Settings command lets you set parameters
for serial communications ports.

Menu Structure

Ports

Settings | Ports...

Steps

Keyboard: ALT-S-O
Shortcut: None
Mouse: Click on Settings menu, then click on
Ports...; or double-click on the Ports icon

Notes

Your computer typically has two serial ports, and
can have as many as four. Each port has
parameters that control how communications with
external devices occur.

The Port Settings command allows you to change
the communications parameters for the four
communications (COM) ports. For each port you
can change the baud rate (110 bps to 19.2 Kbps), the

number of data bits, the parity, the number of stop bits, and the type of flow control used.

Tips

Make sure the communications settings used in Windows match the communications parameters expected by the external device. If they don't, you won't be able to establish a working connection.

Setting port parameters with this command indicates to Windows how it should expect to communicate with a serial printer attached to a specific communications port. If you use other programs that also use the serial ports (such as the Cardfile and Terminal accessories), use those programs to set communications settings as well.

PRINT FILE

File Manager

The Print File command sends a text file to the default printer.

Menu Structure

File | Print...

Steps

Keyboard: ALT-F-P
Shortcut: None
Mouse: Click on File menu, then click on Print...

Notes

The Print File command allows you to print a file
without having to start the application used to
create it. This command is very minimalistic—it
simply copies the file to the printer. There is no
special formatting or handling done with the file.
Thus, this command is only useful for straight text
files (ASCII files). If the file is not a text file, or if
you want to include special formatting, you will
need to use another application program.

When you choose this command, you are asked to
specify the file you want to print. The default is the
file selected in the active directory window. If you
want to select a different file, you enter the filename
here. After entering the filename, the File Manager
sends the specified file to the default printer. If you
need to change the printer, see the Printer Setup
command.

Tips

Do not use this command for printing formatted
word processing documents. The output from your
printer is likely to be gibberish.

PRINT TOPIC

Help System

The Print Topic command copies a major Help
System section to the printer.

Menu Structure

File | Print Topic

Steps

Keyboard: Alt-F-P
Shortcut: None
Mouse: Click on File menu, then click on Print Topic

Notes

The Print Topic command copies a Help System section to your printer. Make sure you have selected and set up the desired printer, either with the Printer Settings command (available from the Control Panel) or with the Printer Setup command (from within the Help System).

PRINTER SETTINGS

Control Panel

The Printer Settings command allows you to select and configure printers connected to your system.

Menu Structure

Printers

Settings | Printers...

Steps

Keyboard: ALT-S-P
Shortcut: None
Mouse: Click on Settings menu, then click on
             Printers...; or double-click on the Printers
             icon

Notes

Besides data communications, printers tend to be
one of the most complicated areas of computing.
When you installed Windows, you had the
opportunity to specify what printers you had and
how they were connected to your computer. After
Windows has been installed, the Printer Settings
command allows you to select a printer (if you have
more than one) and configure it. If you want to add
another printer to your system, you can also do that
with this command.

When you select the Printer Settings command, you
are presented with a list of printers that Windows
believes are connected to your computer. The
heading at the top of this list says "Installed
Printers." The highlighted printer is the one
designated for your system. The Status button
(active or inactive) allows you to manually indicate
whether the printer is available to Windows.

If you choose to configure the selected printer, you
can set port specifications. You can specify where
each printer is to be connected. These connections
can be any of three parallel ports, four serial ports,
an EPT port, or a file. This port setting determines
the destination of the information that Windows
prints. If you choose a serial port, then you should

see the information under the Port Settings
command to be sure your communications settings
are properly set.

From the configuration dialog box, you can select
Setup. This allows you to further define how
Windows should treat the printer you have selected.
Here you can select printer-specific settings that
determine how Windows will control the printer.
Because there are literally hundreds of setup
options for the dozens of printers that could be
connected to Windows, detailed coverage of printer
setup options is beyond the scope of this pocket
reference. For further information in this area, see
Windows 3: The Complete Reference by Tom
Sheldon.

Another important function of this command is that
you can specify whether the Print Manager should
be used with your printer. This is the portion of
Windows that controls the orderly printing of files to
your printer.

Tips

You can print a Windows document for a printer you
don't have connected to your system by directing
output to a file. When you attempt to print, you will
be asked for a filename. Supply one, and Windows
will send information to the file instead of to a
printer. However, the information in the file will
still be formatted for the target printer.

For instance, you might not have a PostScript
printer attached to your computer, but you wish to
produce some PostScript output. When you have
printed the document to the file, you can do the
following:

1. Copy the file to a disk.

2. Take the disk to a computer that has a PostScript printer attached.

3. Using the DOS copy command (or the Windows Copy File command), copy the file to the port to which the printer is connected.

The result is that you will be able to print your document as if the PostScript printer was connected to your system.

PRINTER SETUP

Help System

The Printer Setup command lets you select and set up printers from within the Help System.

Menu Structure

File | Printer Setup...

Steps

Keyboard: ALT-F-R
Shortcut: None
Mouse: Click on File menu, then click on Printer Setup...

Notes

While the primary method of setting up printers is done through the Control Panel command Printer Settings, the Printer Setup command in the Help

System allows you to select an available printer and optionally set it up.

When you select this command, you are shown a list of printers that Windows believes is connected to your system. If the list is incorrect, or if the port assignments for any of the printers is incorrect, you will need to use the Printer Setup command to change them. If the printer you want to use from within the Help System is shown in the list, select it. Then you can click on the Setup button to change specific options that control the printer you have selected.

Because there are literally hundreds of setup options for the dozens of printers that could be connected to Windows, detailed coverage of printer setup options is beyond the scope of this pocket reference. For further information, see *Windows 3: The Complete Reference* by Tom Sheldon.

Tips

If you have only one printer connected to your system and you have already set it up using Printer Settings, you don't need to use the Printer Setup command at all. Printer settings remain constant across Windows applications unless you explicitly change them.

PROPERTIES

Program Manager

The Properties command changes how Windows displays a program group or an application program.

Menu Structure

File | Properties...

Steps

Keyboard: Alt-F-P
Shortcut: None
Mouse: Click on File menu, then click on
Properties...

Notes

When you are ready to use the Properties command,
be sure you have first selected the program group or
application program whose properties you wish to
modify.

If you are changing the properties of an application
program (called a *program item*), then you can
change the description, command line to be
executed, and the icon. The description is the name
that appears under the icon on the desktop, as well
as in the title bar of the window when the
application is running. The command line is the
DOS command Windows executes when the icon is
opened. The icon is the graphic representation of
the application program.

If you minimize a program group window, select it,
and then choose this command, you are given the
opportunity to change the properties assigned to
the whole program group. These properties consist
of the description and the group file designation.
The description is the name that appears under the
icon and at the top of the group window. The group

filename is the DOS file used to define what is
included in this program group.

For more information, see the New command.

REFRESH

File Manager

The Refresh command forces an update of the
directory windows in the File Manager.

Menu Structure

Window | Refresh

Steps

Keyboard: Alt-W-R
Shortcut: F5
Mouse: Click on Window menu, then click on
Refresh

Notes

The File Manager generally does a pretty good job
of reflecting file changes and automatically
updating after every operation. However, if you
have several programs working simultaneously or
you are working in a networked environment, it is
possible for some File Manager windows to not be
updated. If you suspect this has happened, use the
Refresh command. It forces a refresh of the
information displayed in the windows.

Tips

If you are connected to a network, and your computer has been idle for a while, issue the Refresh command. That way you will be sure you are seeing the current state of affairs.

RENAME

File Manager

The Rename command allows you to rename a file or subdirectory.

Menu Structure

File | Rename...

Steps

Keyboard: Alt-F-N
Shortcut: None
Mouse: Click on File menu, then click on
            Rename...

Notes

This command is used to change the name of either a file or subdirectory. When you choose the command, you are shown the old name for the item and asked to enter a new name. The currently selected item is shown as a default for the old name. If the old name is incorrect, you can move the text cursor and change it.

Once you have verified the old name and provided a new name, click on the Rename button. The change will be completed.

If a file has the read-only attribute enabled, it cannot be renamed without first disabling the attribute. For more information on attributes, see the Change Attributes command.

REPLACE ON OPEN

File Manager

The Replace on Open command instructs the File Manager to reuse directory windows instead of opening new ones.

Menu Structure

View | Replace on Open

Steps

Keyboard: Alt-V-R
Shortcut: None
Mouse: Click on View menu, then click on Replace on Open

Notes

This is a toggle option, meaning that the same command turns the option on and off. When you select the command the first time, automatic window replacement is activated and a check mark appears beside the command on the menu. Select

Replace on Open again, and the check mark disappears.

Normally, as you work with the File Manager you can end up with many, many directory windows open on your screen at the same time. This command allows you to change that. If Replace on Open is enabled, Windows will automatically reuse a directory window when you change directories, rather than opening a new one. The net effect is fewer windows cluttering your desktop.

RESTORE WINDOW

System-wide

The Restore Window command restores the current window to its normal size.

Menu Structure

Control | Restore

Steps

Keyboard: ALT-DASH-R for a document window, ALT-SPACEBAR-R for all other windows
Shortcut: None
Mouse: Click on the Control menu, then click on Restore

Notes

The Control menu is accessed through the icon in the upper-left corner of a window.

For readers who are not using a mouse, this is the command provided to restore a window to an "in between" size—it is neither minimized nor maximized. It is the size created with your last sizing operation. The resulting window can be resized using the Size Window command. This command is only available if the window has either been minimized or maximized.

Tips

If you are using a mouse and the window is maximized, simply click on the icon containing both an upward- and downward-pointing arrow. This icon is near the upper-right corner of the window.

If you are using a mouse, and the window is minimized, simply double-click on the icon to restore.

RUN

Program Manager or File Manager

The Run command allows you to run an application program.

Menu Structure

File | Run...

Steps

Keyboard: Alt-F-R
Shortcut: None
Mouse: Click on File menu, then click on Run...

Notes

This is one method used to run programs within Windows. When you choose this command, you are asked to enter a command line. This is the name of the program you want to run, followed by any parameters that the program may require. When you press ENTER, Windows will attempt to load and execute the program.

If you check the box that says "Run Minimized," then the program is started and automatically minimized. It will then appear as an icon at the bottom of your desktop.

The Run command is the same as using the Open command with the program icon selected.

Tips

If you are using a mouse, there are two additional ways you can start a program. First, you can double-click on the icon for the program. This is a fast, efficient way to begin a program that has been set up for use with Windows. If you are in the File Manager, you can also double-click on a PIF, EXE, or COM file to begin an application.

Second, if you are in the File Manager you can drag the icon for a data file on top of the icon for the program that will use the data file. Windows will attempt to load the program and the data file.

SAVE AS

Clipboard

The Save As command saves the contents of the Clipboard to a disk file.

Menu Structure

File | Save As...

Steps

Keyboard: Alt-F-A
Shortcut: None
Mouse: Click on File menu, then click on Save As...

Notes

The Save As command allows you to save whatever is in the Clipboard to a special Clipboard disk file. Clipboard files are saved with the extension CLP. When you choose this command you are prompted for a filename. You only need to enter up to eight characters for a filename; the CLP file extension is added automatically.

Anything that can be stored in the Clipboard can be saved with this command. Information is put into and taken out of the Clipboard with editing commands, the most common of which are Copy, Cut, and Paste.

The Clipboard is not cleared at the end of this command. If you want to clear the clipboard to free up memory, you should use the Delete Clipboard command.

Also see the Open Clipboard File command.

Tips

If you find yourself pasting the same graphic (such as a logo or special symbol) again and again, copy it into the Clipboard and save it to disk. Then you can access the file at a later date and paste it into whatever you are working on at the time.

You can copy an entire Windows screen into the Clipboard simply by pressing the PRINTSCREEN key. You can then save the file to disk or paste it into a graphics program.

You can copy the active window into the Clipboard by pressing ALT-PRINTSCREEN.

It is a good idea to devise Clipboard filenames that indicate what is in the file. For instance, you might want graphics files to end in the characters GR. The code you devise is up to you.

SEARCH

Help System

A button in the Help System that allows you to search for specific information among the topics available in the current Help System file.

Menu Structure

Steps

Keyboard: ALT-S
Shortcut: None
Mouse: Click on Search button

Notes

The Help System built into Windows is very powerful. It displays information from a help file in a consistent and clear manner. These help files have the HLP file extension. If, when you access the Help System, Windows discovers that there is a help file that has the same root filename as the application program that is currently active, that help file is opened and ready for use.

Whoever designed the help file currently being used also decided what the major keywords were in the help file. These keywords are directly accessible with the Search command.

When you select this command, the following window will appear:

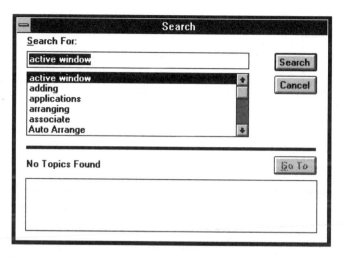

From this screen you can specify what you are searching for. The word you enter is called a *keyword*. As you type the keyword, the alphabetical list of keywords displayed under where you are typing will be updated so that the first letters of the top keyword shown matches the first letters of what you have typed. This means you don't have to type the whole word. You just have to type enough to be able to distinguish your keyword from all the other keywords available for the current help file.

When you click on the Search button or press ENTER you will be shown a list of the topics that include the keyword you entered. Then you can jump directly to any of the sections you desire. You can either highlight the topic and click on the Go To button, or you can double-click on the topic desired.

Tips

If you are unfamiliar with the subject matter and don't know the proper keyword to enter, you can browse through the available keywords by using the scroll bar to the right of the alphabetical keyword list.

SEARCH FOR FILES

File Manager

The Search for Files command lets you search for a specific file in either the current directory or over an entire disk.

Menu Structure

File | Search...

Steps

Keyboard: ALT-F-H
Shortcut: None
Mouse: Click on File menu, then click on Search...

Notes

When you choose this command, you are asked to provide a file specification for which to search. You can specify partial names or get really fancy with this parameter. Full discussion of filenames and wildcard characters is beyond the scope of this pocket reference. For more information, see *Simply*

DOS or *DOS: The Complete Reference, Third Edition*, both by Kris Jamsa and published by Osborne/McGraw-Hill.

When you specify a filename template, the File Manager begins searching for files that match. When the search is complete, a window called Search Results is created, and all the located files are listed in it. If you directed the search to occur on the entire disk, then full path names are shown for the files.

Using the Search Results window, you can act on these files as if they were in a single directory. This allows for some very powerful operations to occur. For instance, if you have Excel spreadsheet files in various places all over your hard drive, you could search for all files ending in XLS. The File Manager will list all these files as a result of the search. Then you could move all these files to a single directory, or to another drive. The result is a quick and easy way to clean up your hard drive.

SELECT ALL

File Manager

The Select All command lets you select all files within the current directory window.

Menu Structure

File | Select All

Steps

Keyboard: ALT-F-S
Shortcut: CTRL-/
Mouse: Click on File menu, then click on Select
        All

Notes

The Select All command is only available when a
directory window is open and selected; it is not
available from the directory tree. When you use this
command, all of the files in the current directory are
selected and highlighted. This command is
generally used in preparation for some other
operation such as copying, moving, or deleting.

Also see the Deselect All command.

SELECTED NET QUEUE

Print Manager

The Selected Net Queue displays the queue status
for a network print queue.

Menu Structure

View | Selected Net Queue...

Steps

Keyboard: Alt-V-S
Shortcut: None
Mouse: Click on View menu, then click on
Selected Net Queue...

Notes

The Selected Net Queue command is available only
if you are connected to a network and using printing
facilities for that network. Also, you will only be
able to use this command for network printers you
are connected to. You connect to network printers
by using the Printer Settings command from the
Control Panel.

If the currently selected printer happens to be a
network print queue, this command allows you to
view a list of the print jobs waiting in the queue.
This lets you see how your print jobs are
progressing.

A network print queue is different than the print
queue maintained by the Print Manager. The Print
Manager maintains a queue of print jobs for your
computer alone. A network print queue is for the
print jobs of all users attached to the network.

SET UP APPLICATIONS

Setup

The Set Up Applications command automatically
adds program icons to Windows for your
applications.

Menu Structure

Options | Set Up Applications...

Steps

Keyboard: ALT-O-S
Shortcut: None
Mouse: Click on Options menu, then click on Set Up Applications...

Notes

When you first installed Windows, you were given the option of having the installation program search through your hard drives to find application programs to install in Windows. The Set Up Applications command does the same thing. It allows you to search through any drive for applications that Windows recognizes and can install automatically.

If you did this when you installed Windows, you should only have to do it again if you make significant changes to the programs on your system. When you choose this command, you are asked to specify which drive or drives should be searched. Once this is done, the Setup program searches the drives for programs it may recognize. You will then have the option of adding those programs to the system.

If you add a program, Windows will create an icon for it and add it to the Program Manager. If you choose to add a program that has previously been added, you will have two identical icons in the Program Manager that both do the same thing. To

remove one you will need to use the Delete
command from the Program Manager.

SIZE WINDOW

System-wide

The Size Window command restores the current
window to its normal size.

Menu Structure

Control | Size

Steps

Keyboard: Alt-Dash-S for a document window, Alt-
Spacebar-S for all other windows
Shortcut: None
Mouse: Click on the Control menu, then click on
Size

Notes

The Control menu is accessed through the icon in
the upper-left corner of a window.

For readers who are not using a mouse, this is the
command provided to change the size of a window.
When you choose the command, a multitipped
arrow pointing in four directions appears. Press any
of the following cursor control keys for the desired
action:

Left Arrow   The left arrow moves the left border
of the window. The other borders stay in place.

Right Arrow   The right arrow moves the right border of the window. The other borders stay in place.

Up Arrow   The upward-pointing arrow moves the top border of the window. The other borders stay in place.

Down Arrow   The downward-pointing arrow moves the bottom border of the window. The other borders stay in place.

If you want to move a corner of the window, press two arrow keys simultaneously. For instance, if you want to move the window's lower-right corner, press the right and down arrows at the same time.

Once you have selected the border you want to move, use the arrow keys to move it in the direction desired. When you are satisfied with the move, press the Enter key. If you press Esc, the sizing will be canceled.

The Size Window command is not available if the window has been minimized.

Tips

If you are using a mouse, click along any border of the window, or at any corner, and drag the border to the new position desired. This performs the same task as the Size Window command.

SOUND SETTINGS

Control Panel

The Sound Settings command turns the warning beep on or off.

Menu Structure

Sound

Settings | Sound...

Steps

Keyboard: ALT-S-S
Shortcut: None
Mouse: Click on Settings menu, then click on Sound...; or double-click on the Sound icon

Notes

When Windows detects an error, it sounds an audible alert to draw your attention to the error. If you want to turn the sound off (or back on—this is a toggle), you can do so with this command.

STATUS BAR

File Manager

The Status Bar command controls whether the status bar at the bottom of the File Manager window is displayed.

Menu Structure

Options | Status Bar

Steps

Keyboard: ALT-O-S
Shortcut: None
Mouse: Click on Options menu, then click on Status Bar

Notes

This is a toggle option that is normally enabled. A toggle option is simply one that can be turned on and off with the same command. When you select the Status Bar command the first time, the status bar at the bottom of the File Manager window disappears and the check mark beside the command on the menu disappears. Select the Status Bar command again, and the status bar and menu check mark reappear.

With the Status Bar option turned on, the File Manager can provide more detailed information about the status of your work. Normally, it is used to display a message indicating the result of the last operation. If you feel comfortable without such

information, or if the status bar bothers you, then
turn it off.

The use of this command is a personal preference.
It does not affect the overall functioning of
Windows.

SWITCH TO

System-wide

The Switch To command lets you select, end, and
organize currently running tasks.

Menu Structure

Control | Switch to...

Steps

Keyboard: ALT–SPACEBAR–W
Shortcut: CTRL–ESC
Mouse: Click on Control menu, then click on
Switch to...

Notes

The Control menu is accessed through the icon in
the upper-left corner of a window.

This command is used to switch between tasks.
Tasks are individual programs running under
Windows. When you choose this command, you are
presented with a list of the currently executing
tasks. You can select a task and press ENTER, double-
click on a task, or click on a task and click on the

Switch To button, and that task will be switched to the foreground. You can also terminate programs using this command by selecting a task and then clicking on the End Task button.

You can choose the Cascade, Tile, or Arrange Icons options from this command to perform the same functions in relation to the tasks as you do when using them as individual commands.

Tip

If you are using a mouse, you can double-click on the desktop (outside of any windows) in order to access the Task List. This is the same as using the Switch To command.

TILE WINDOWS

Program Manager or File Manager

The Tile Windows command arranges the open document windows in a side-by-side fashion.

Menu Structure

Window | Tile

Steps

Keyboard: ALT-W-T
Shortcut: SHIFT-F4
Mouse: Click on Window menu, then click on Tile

Notes

If you get several windows open on your screen at
once, it can quickly become cluttered. If you choose
this command, Windows will, within the available
desktop space, rearrange the windows so they are
side-by-side with each other.

When tiling the windows, they are resized and, if
Auto Arrange is enabled, the icons are rearranged
in each window. The following shows a sample
screen after tiling:

UPDATE NET QUEUES

Print Manager

The Update Net Queues command forces an update
of the network printer queue status display.

Menu Structure

View | Update Net Queues

Steps

Keyboard: Alt-V-U
Shortcut: None
Mouse: Click on View menu, then click on
Update Net Queues

Notes

This command is available only if you are connected
to a network and using printing facilities for that
network.

The Print Manager generally does a pretty good job
of reflecting changes and updating network printer
queues, particularly ones to which you are attached.
However, if you have several programs working
simultaneously or network traffic is very heavy, it is
possible that the status of the queues may not be
updated. If you suspect this has happened, use the
Update Net Queues command. It forces a refresh of
the information displayed in the print queue status
windows.

This command is also necessary if you have turned
off Network Display Updating using the Network
Options command.

VIEW BY NAME

File Manager

The View By Name command directs the File
Manager to display files sorted by their names
within the current directory window.

Menu Structure

View | By Name

Steps

Keyboard: ALT-V-B
Shortcut: None
Mouse: Click on View menu, then click on By
Name

Notes

This is a toggle option, meaning that the same
command turns the option on and off. When you
select the command, a check mark appears beside
the command on the menu. Select a different
sorting option, and the check mark disappears.

When View By Name is selected, the File Manager
sorts the files in the current directory window by
name. This is the normal sorting order for the File
Manager. For other sorting methods, see the View
By Type and View Sort By commands.

VIEW BY TYPE

File Manager

Directs the File Manager to display files within the current directory window sorted by filename extension.

Menu Structure

View | By Type

Steps

Keyboard: ALT-V-T
Shortcut: None
Mouse: Click on View menu, then click on By Type

Notes

This is a toggle option, meaning that the same command turns the option on and off. When you select the command, a check mark appears beside the command on the menu. Select a different sorting option, and the check mark disappears.

When View By Type is selected, the File Manager sorts the directory displays first by filename extension, and then by filename within extension group. This sorting order is very handy, because it clusters files by type. This makes it easier to work with file commands like Copy File or Delete.

For other sorting methods, see the View By Name and View Sort By commands.

VIEW FILE DETAILS

File Manager

The View File Details command directs the File
Manager to display full details of files in the current
window.

Menu Structure

View | File Details

Steps

Keyboard: Alt-V-F
Shortcut: None
Mouse: Click on View menu, then click on File
Details

Notes

This is a toggle option, meaning that the same
command turns the option on and off. When you
select the command, a check mark appears beside
the command on the menu. Select a different
viewing option, and the check mark disappears.

When View File Details is selected, the File
Manager displays full information on each file in a
subdirectory. The information displayed includes
the filename, its size, date and time of creation, and
the file attributes enabled for the file. The date and
time displayed for a file indicates the last time the
file was *changed*, not the last time it was accessed.

The file attributes display may have nothing but lines to the right side of a file entry, or there may be the letters R, H, S, or A instead of lines. These letters indicate the properties, or *attributes*, possessed by the file. Normally you won't see files with the H or S attributes displayed; this can be changed with the View Include command. For more information on file attributes, see the Change Attributes command.

For other display modes, see the View Name and View Other commands.

Tips

If there are a lot of files in a directory, you can spend less time scrolling the screen by using the View By Name command. This command displays multiple columns of files on the screen, where other viewing commands display only a single column but more information about individual files.

VIEW INCLUDE

File Manager

The View Include command specifies which files should be displayed by the File Manager.

Menu Structure

View | Include...

Steps

Keyboard: Alt-V-C
Shortcut: None
Mouse: Click on View menu, then click on
              Include...

Notes

With the View Include command you can specify
the name and type of files to be displayed. In
addition, you can select whether system and hidden
files are displayed.

The Name box allows you to indicate a template
that will be used to determine which files get
displayed. Normally, this is set to *.*, the DOS
wildcard characters, which indicate that any named
files should be listed. You can specify partial names
or get really fancy with this parameter. Full
discussion of filenames and wildcard characters is
beyond the scope of this pocket reference. For more
information, see *Simply DOS* or *DOS: The Complete
Reference, Third Edition*, both by Kris Jamsa.

The File Type box lists the file types that can be
displayed by the File Manager. You can select
which ones are displayed and which ones aren't.
The possibilities are

Directories   If the Directories option is selected,
then directories are included in file displays.

Programs   If the Programs option is selected,
then files with the EXE, COM, BAT, or PIF file
extension are included in file displays.

Documents   If the Documents option is selected, then files associated with programs are displayed. See the Associate File command for more information.

Other Files   If the Other Files option is selected, then non-program and non-document files are included in file displays.

If you specify that system and hidden files are displayed, then they are included in file listings.

All changes with this command affect only the current File Manager window, unless you check the box that says "Set System Default." Doing so causes your changes to have universal effect across all File Manager operations.

VIEW NAME

File Manager

The View Name command directs the File Manager to display files in the current window with only the filename showing.

Menu Structure

View | Name

Steps

Keyboard: Alt-V-N
Shortcut: None
Mouse: Click on View menu, then click on Name

Notes

This is a toggle option, meaning that the same command turns the option on and off. When you select the command, a check mark appears beside the command on the menu. Select a different viewing option, and the check mark disappears.

When View Name is selected, the File Manager only displays filenames when showing the contents of directories. This is the normal display mode for the File Manager. For other display modes, see the View File Details and View Other commands.

Tips

If there are a lot of files in a directory, you can spend less time scrolling the screen by using the View Name command. This command displays three columns of files on the screen, where other viewing commands display only a single column.

VIEW OTHER

File Manager

The View Name command lets you control what information the File Manager displays about files in the current window.

Menu Structure

View | Other...

Steps

Keyboard: Alt-V-O
Shortcut: None
Mouse: Click on View menu, then click on
             Other...

Notes

When you select this option, you are presented with
a list of four items which control what information
the File Manager displays about files. The list
includes the following options:

Size   With this option selected, the size of each
file, in bytes, is displayed.

Last Modification Date   If enabled, this option
indicates the date when a change was last made
to the file.

Last Modification Time   This option controls
whether the File Manager shows the time of day
when the last change was made to the file.

File Flags   These flags indicate the attributes of
the file. These attributes are the properties
possessed by the file, and can be changed with
the Change Attributes command.

Any changes made with this command affect only
the window in which you are working. You can
make your settings the default for all windows by
enabling the Set System Default option.

For other display modes, see the View File Details
and View Name commands.

Tips

If you enable all details for a file, it is the same as using the View File Details command.

Normally you won't see files with the H or S attributes displayed; this can be changed with the View Include command.

VIEW SORT BY

File Manager

The View Sort By command allows you to specify how the File Manager should sort the filenames in the current window.

Menu Structure

View | Sort by...

Steps

Keyboard: Alt-V-S
Shortcut: None
Mouse: Click on View menu, then click on Sort by...

Notes

The File Manager allows you to sort files in any of four different ways. You can sort file displays by filename, type, file size, or modification date. Each of these options has the following effect:

Name   With the Name option, files are sorted in ascending order based on the filename.

Type   With the Type option, files are sorted in ascending order based first on filename extension, and then on filename within extension.

Size   With the Size option, Files are sorted in descending order based on file size.

Modification Date   With the Modification Date option, files are sorted in descending order (reverse chronological order) based on the date they were last *changed* (not last opened).

Regardless of the method you use to sort your files, directories always appear at the beginning of the sorted list.

If you select the Set System Default option, then the sorting order you select is used for all File Manager directory windows, not just the current one.

Tips

If you want to sort by name or type, use the View By Name or View By Type commands. It is faster than using this command.

Task Reference

This section provides a quick overview of common tasks, and how they are accomplished in Windows 3. Every attempt has been made to make the task names as short and simple as possible so you can find the operation you need to perform even if you have no idea what the command name might be.

The discussions under these tasks include the use of many commands. You can look up these commands in the Command Reference section for a full description of each.

Tasks are arranged in alphabetical order. The heading for each task is presented in the following manner:

TASK NAME

Following each heading is a question that puts the task into a context that many users might face. The purpose of these questions is to focus your own ideas about how each task could apply to your use of Windows.

Notes

Following the introductory question is the *Notes* category. This section gives the answer to the question in a discussion that attempts to promote a fuller understanding of solutions for the task.

Pertinent Commands

Next is a category called *Pertinent Commands*.
These are the commands that perform the task at
hand, along with the program from which the
command is available. Once you know which
commands perform the task you're about to
undertake, you may wish to refer to the Command
Reference for further information about how
Windows operates in relation to that task.

Related Tasks

The next category is called *Related Tasks*. This
cross references commands within this Task
Reference. It lists other tasks that are related to the
one under discussion.

Suggestions

Finally, some tasks include a category called
Suggestions. These are additional pointers or tips
that you may find helpful in dealing with situations
where the task may apply.

For a complete list of tasks in this section, see the
Contents. Since the wording used for tasks is
discretionary, you might not word a task in the
same manner as was chosen for this section. The
following list is intended as a cross-reference of
alternate wording for some tasks:

If You Want to:	See the Task:
Add a command	Adding Applications
Add a program	Adding Applications
Add a program group	Creating New Program Groups

If You Want to:	See the Task:
Build a selection set	Selecting Multiple Files
Cancel a print job	Deleting a Print Job
Change colors	Changing Desktop Colors
Change date and time	Setting the Date and Time
Change a filename	Renaming a File
Change paper orientation	Setting Paper Orientation
Change a program name	Renaming a Program
Change your keyboard	Changing Your Equipment
Change your monitor	Changing Your Equipment
Choose a printer	Changing Printers
Choose a window	Selecting Windows
Create a bootable disk	Making a System Disk
Create a selection set	Selecting Multiple Files
Create a system disk	Making a System Disk
Delete an application	Deleting a Program
Duplicate a disk	Copying a Disk
Duplicate a file	Copying a File
Duplicate a program icon	Copying a Program
End a program	Stopping a Program
Erase a file	Deleting a File
Erase a program	Deleting a Program
Exit Windows	Ending Windows
Make a bootable disk	Making a System Disk
Make a directory	Creating a Directory
Make a window bigger	Maximizing Windows *or* Changing Window Sizes
Make a window smaller	Minimizing Windows *or* Changing Window Sizes
Pick a window	Selecting Windows
Quit Windows	Ending Windows
Remove a print job	Deleting a Print Job
Set landscape mode	Setting Paper Orientation
Set portrait mode	Setting Paper Orientation

ADDING APPLICATIONS

How do I add applications to run from the Program Manager in Windows?

Notes

There are three ways to add commands to the Program Manager in Windows:

- Use the Set Up Applications command from the Setup program. This is perhaps the easiest method of adding programs to Windows.

- Add applications manually. This involves using the New command from the Program Manager and possibly the PIF editor. This is the most difficult way to add applications (and sometimes the only way).

- Use a third-party install program. This is a common method when installing a program written specifically for Windows 3. The installation program takes care of any PIF files, adding program items, and possibly adding program groups. These installation programs vary widely and depend on the good graces of the vendor supplying your new software.

Pertinent Commands

Set Up Applications, Setup
New, Program Manager
Properties, Program Manager

Related Tasks

Creating New Program Groups
Running a Program
Stopping a Program

Suggestions

If you are installing new sofware, check with the vendor to see if they have a special installation program for Windows 3.

Try using the Set Up Applications command to see if it can recognize and install the software you want added.

ADDING A PRINTER

I have just purchased a new printer. How do I get it to work with Windows?

Notes

The first step in adding a printer is to connect it to your computer. Generally, it will either connect to the parallel or serial port. You will need the proper cable to do this; the place where you got your printer should be able to supply one.

Since hardware lessons and cabling diagrams are a little outside the scope of this pocket reference, if you are having problems so far you should refer to another book. *Upgrading PCs Made Easy* by Bud and Alex Aaron, published by Osborne/McGraw-Hill, is a good choice.

Once your printer is connected to your computer, go ahead and start Windows 3. Go to the Control Panel and select the Printers icon (see the Printer Settings command for more information). Click on the button that says Add Printer... This will allow you to load the proper printer driver for your new printer. Scroll through the list of available printers, and select the one that most closely approximates your printer. Click on the Install button and Windows will inform you if it needs a disk from which to load the printer driver. The drivers for all the printers in the Add Printer list are on the original Windows software disks.

Now that the printer driver is installed, you need to click on the Configure button. This allows you to specify the printer port used by your new printer. Select the same port to which you connected your printer earlier. When you click on OK, your printer should be ready to use with Windows. If it doesn't work, check the following:

- Is the printer status set to Active?
- Does the printer port in Windows match the port to which the printer is actually connected?
- Are the physical cable connections tight?

Pertinent Commands

Printer Settings, Control Panel

Related Tasks

Changing Printers
Changing the Default Printer
Removing a Printer

Suggestions

If you continue to have problems making your printer work, try printing something to it from DOS (outside of Windows). If you are able to do this, then you can assume that the problem is not with the printer itself, but in how Windows is set up to access the printer.

CHANGING THE DEFAULT PRINTER

Some of my applications only print to the default printer. How do I determine what the default printer is, and how do I change it?

Notes

Some applications will simply only print to the default printer. For instance, when you print a file from the File Manager, it is directed to the default printer.

You can determine your default printer by opening the Printers icon from the Control Panel. The default printer is listed near the lower-left corner of the dialog box. To change the default printer, double-click on one of the installed printers listed in the upper-left corner of the dialog box. This should change the default printer.

Pertinent Commands

Printer Settings, Control Panel

Related Tasks

Adding a Printer
Changing Printers

CHANGING DESKTOP COLORS

How do I change the colors used by Windows?

Notes

Changing colors is an easy thing to do. To change the colors of your desktop, open the Colors icon from the Control Panel. There you can experiment and see how the colors will look before you make them permanent.

Windows comes with several color combinations already saved (see the Color command for more information). If you are so motivated, you can also save your favorite color combinations. That way you can call them up again at a later date. To save color combinations, you will need to use the Color Palette to change the menu colors. When you are happy with how they appear, click on the Save Scheme button and provide a name for the color scheme.

Pertinent Commands

Color Settings, Control Panel

CHANGING DIRECTORIES

How do I change directories?

Notes

If you are familar with DOS and understand the basics of subdirectories, this may seem a natural question to ask. Basically, when you are outside of an application program, there is no need to change directories in Windows. Once you are in a program, it is up to the program to handle making directory changes.

The most common need to change directories is within the File Manager. Here you can traverse directories quickly and easily using the Directory Tree. You change directories by simply clicking on an icon that represents the directory you want. You can also use the cursor control keys to move through the directories.

Pertinent Commands

Replace on Open, File Manager

Related Task

Changing the Drive
Creating a Directory

Suggestions

You can open, view, and access multiple directories by simply opening the desired directories from the

Directory Tree. Each time you open a directory, a new directory window is created. These windows can be arranged on the desktop so you can quickly and easily work across directories.

Note that you will not be able to open multiple directory windows if you have enabled the Replace on Open command.

CHANGING THE DRIVE

How do I change the drive?

Notes

Changing drives and *specifying* drives are two different things. There are many places where you will need to specify a drive. For instance, you specify a drive when you are adding an application and you need to include a drive name on the command line designation, or when you are installing applications using the Setup program and it asks which drives should be searched.

There is generally only one place where you may need to change drives, however. That is in the File Manager. To change drives here, simply click on the button representing the disk drive. If you have a question about what type of disk drive it is, the icons will generally let you know. The following are three types of Windows drives:

Floppy drive

Hard drive

Network drive

As you navigate through drives and directories, Windows will keep you informed about what is happening.

The ability to change drives while using an application depends on the application. For more information, consult the documentation for the application you are using.

Pertinent Commands

Connect Net Drive, File Manager
Disconnect Net Drive, File Manager

Related Tasks

Changing Directories

CHANGING THE KEYBOARD REPEAT RATE

When I am typing, I find that many of the keys I press are actually appearing twice on the screen. How do I correct this?

Notes

Windows allows you to control what is called the *key repeat rate*. This is the relative length of time that you must hold down a key before it repeats. The faster the key repeat rate, the shorter the time you have to release a key before it repeats.

If you are a slow, methodical typist, then you may need to change the key repeat rate to a slower setting. This is done by using the Keyboard Settings command from the Control Panel. When you use this command, you will be able to adjust the key repeat rate. Try sliding the block toward the left. This will cause the key repeat rate to slow down.

Note that the key repeat rate affects all keys on your keyboard, including the cursor control keys. Thus, if you slow down the key repeat rate, the arrow keys will respond slower when you hold them down.

Pertinent Commands

Keyboard Settings, Control Panel

Related Topics

Changing Your Equipment

Suggestions

If you have the key repeat rate set at the lowest setting, and you still get double keys on the screen, you could be suffering from what is called "key bounce." This is a condition caused by your computer's keyboard, not by Windows itself. Key bounce can usually only be corrected by getting a new keyboard. If you change keyboards, you may have to change the equipment settings that Windows uses for your keyboard.

CHANGING PRINTERS

I have multiple printers attached to my system. How do I change which printer is currently being used?

Notes

Any answer to this question assumes you already have installed the printer and that Windows is aware that the printer is available. If not, see the related discussion under the task Adding a Printer.

There are several ways you can change which printer you want to use. The first, and most common way is with the Control Panel. Go to the Control Panel and open the Printers icon. Here you can select which printer is the current printer by clicking on the printer name in the upper-left corner of the dialog box. Then make sure the status for the printer is set to Active, and click on OK. That's all there is to it.

The other ways to select printers depend on the application programs you are using. For instance, it is possible in Write (the Windows accessory) to use the Printer Setup command on the File menu to select which printer should be used. Only the printers that have an active status will be displayed. Many other programs offer similar abilities.

Pertinent Commands

Printer Settings, Control Panel
Printer Setup, Help System

Related Tasks

Adding a Printer
Changing the Default Printer

CHANGING WINDOW SIZES

How do I change the size of a window?

Notes

The easiest way to change the size of the window is with the mouse. As you move the mouse cursor near the border of the active window, you will notice that the arrow changes to a double arrow. This represents the direction in which you can move that particular border. If you move the cursor near the corner of the window, you will notice that the double arrow points diagonally. This means you can affect two of the borders at the same time.

In order to change the window size with the mouse, move the mouse cursor to the border or corner you wish to change. Then click the left mouse button and, while holding it down, drag the border to the desired position. When you let go of the button, the window is resized.

If you are using the keyboard, the process is a little more intricate. You must first choose the Size command from the Control menu, and then press an arrow key to designate which border you wish to move. If you want to move a corner, you can press two arrow keys simultaneously.

Once you have selected a border or corner to move, use the arrow keys to move it. When you are satisfied with the new position, press ENTER. If you change your mind and don't want to resize the window, press ESC.

You also need to be aware that certain commands change the size of the windows automatically. For instance, the Tile Windows or Cascade Windows commands affect all the windows on the screen.

Pertinent Commands

Cascade Windows, Program Manager *or* File
   Manager
Size Window, System-wide
Switch To, System-wide
Tile Windows, Program Manager *or* File Manager

CHANGING YOUR EQUIPMENT

I've just added a new piece of equipment that I want to use with Windows. How do I do this?

Notes

There are many pieces of equipment that you can take advantage of with Windows. These include monitors, hard drives, printers, modems, mice, networks, keyboards, and the like. Actually, if you change monitors, there is nothing you need to do in relation to Windows; the change comes in if you change the type of display card you are using—for instance, if you upgrade from an EGA card to a VGA card.

If you are changing your display card, keyboard, mouse, or network, use the Change System Settings command to make Windows aware of your new equipment.

If you have added an additional hard drive or a new modem, there is nothing you have to do in relation to Windows itself. Windows should automatically recognize the hard drive. You may need to make changes in your application programs, however, as these exert further control over these types of devices.

If you are changing or adding a printer, you can use the Printer Settings command. For more information on this, see the Adding a Printer task.

Pertinent Commands

Change System Settings, Setup
Printer Settings, Control Panel

Related Tasks

Adding a Printer

Suggestions

If you are changing your display system to an older type (for instance, from VGA to EGA), make sure you make your display changes in Windows *before* you actually change the hardware. If you don't, you won't be able to use Windows. The VGA video drivers used by Windows will not work with EGA displays.

COPYING A DISK

I want to copy a disk. How do I do it?

Notes

How you copy a disk depends, in large part, on what you are copying *from* and *to*. If you are copying between diskettes that both have the same capacity, you can use any of the following methods:

- Within the File Manager, use the Copy Diskette command.

- Within the File Manager, use the Format Diskette command to format a blank disk, and then use the Copy File command to copy the files to the new diskette.

- From the DOS prompt, use the DISKCOPY command. This is a DOS command, and beyond the scope of this pocket reference. But access to the command is available from Windows. For more information on this command, refer to *DOS: The Complete Reference, Third Edition*, by Kris Jamsa, published by Osborne/McGraw-Hill.

If you need to copy between diskettes that have differing capacities, then only the second option can be used.

Pertinent Commands

Copy Diskette, File Manager
Copy File, File Manager
Format Diskette, File Manager

Related Tasks

Copying a File
Formatting a Disk

Suggestions

Make sure that the disk onto which you will be copying is blank. The copy commands (particularly those that copy an entire diskette) are destructive in nature. This means that files on the destination disk could be overwritten by the operation.

COPYING A FILE

How do I copy my spreadsheet file to diskette?

Notes

Copying a file is a simple process, whether you are copying to another directory, another hard disk, or a floppy diskette. All the file copying capabilities of Windows lie within the File Manager.

Once in the File Manager, select the file or files you wish to copy. Then, use the Copy File command to specify where you want to copy the files. If you are using a mouse, open both the source and destination directories as individual windows. Then you can drag the files to be copied to their new location.

If you are not using a mouse, you must use the Copy File command and enter the complete path for the destination of the files to be copied. While this may

sound difficult, it is pretty easy as long as you have
a firm handle on where the files should end up.

Pertinent Commands

Copy File, File Manager
Format Diskette, File Manager
Search for Files, File Manager
Select All, File Manager

Related Tasks

Copying a Disk
Copying a Program
Formatting a Disk
Moving a File
Searching for Files
Selecting Multiple Files

Suggestions

If you are copying to a floppy diskette, make sure it
is formatted before you start. You cannot copy files
to a diskette that has not been formatted.

Suppose your file copying needs are as follows:

1. There are at least two files to be copied.

2. The files are in different subdirectories.

3. All the files have the same extension (the
    characters in the filename following the
    period).

This is not an unusual scenario. If you find yourself
in this situation, use the Search for Files command
to build a selection set of the files that have the
common extension. Then use the Select All

command to select all those files, and finally the Copy File command to copy these to the destination.

COPYING A PROGRAM

How do I copy a program in one window of the Program Manager to another?

Notes

Copying a program is similar to copying a file, except all operations occur in the Program Manager. First, you need to select the program icon you wish to copy. Then, use the Copy command to specify the program group that you want to copy the program to. If you are using a mouse, open both the source and destination program groups as individual windows. Then, while holding down the CTRL key, you can drag the icon to be copied to its new location.

If you are not using a mouse, you must use the Copy command and enter the name of the program group to receive the copy. If you can't remember the names of all the program groups, you can browse through them by clicking on the arrow at the right of the default group.

Pertinent Commands

Copy Program Item, Program Manager

Related Tasks

Copying a File
Moving a Program

CREATING A DIRECTORY

How do I add a new directory on my hard drive?

Notes

Adding a new directory is a common occurrence in DOS computing. To do this, you use the Create Directory command in the File Manager. When you use this command, you will be prompted for the name of the directory to add. Names should follow the same rules as names for files; they should be eight characters or less with up to three characters for an extension. The extension should be separated from the rest of the filename by a period. If you don't want the directory to be added within the current directory, you must provide a complete path name of the directory to add.

Pertinent Commands

Create Directory, File Manager

CREATING NEW PROGRAM GROUPS

I don't like the way some of my programs are grouped in the Program Manager. How do I create new groups and add programs to them?

Notes

Creating new program groups in the Program Manager is quite easy. You can use the New command from the Program Manager to do this.

When you issue the command, make sure you then specify that you are adding a program group.

You can give program groups any name you wish. However, your desktop will appear less cluttered if you keep each name relatively short. (The words under the program group icons tend to run together if the names are too long.)

Once you have provided a description for the new group, press ENTER. That's it. You have just added a new program group. At this point it will appear as an open window, and you can move applications into it as you please by dragging icons from other program groups. Remember to hold down the CTRL key if you want to copy icons to the new program group.

Pertinent Commands

New, Program Manager
Properties, Program Manager

Related Tasks

Adding Applications

Suggestions

If you would rather change the title of a current program group, you can use the Properties command. This eliminates the need to add a group, transfer all the files into it, and then delete the old group.

DELETING A FILE

I've been wanting to free up some disk space lately, but don't know how to delete my old files. How do I do this?

Notes

Deleting files is a common occurrence. There are a couple of ways to do it with Windows.

First, you can use the File Manager's Delete command. This allows you to delete one or more files, or an entire subdirectory. All you need to do is select the files or directories you wish to delete, and then either invoke the Delete command or, better yet, press the Del key. Windows will make sure you really want to delete the files before continuing.

If you would rather not see the promptings before each file is deleted, use the Confirmation Options command to change this.

You may not be able to delete some of your files. If you have files with the read-only, system, or hidden attributes enabled, you won't be able to delete them. If you do want to delete them, use the Change Attributes command to disable all the attributes of the file before trying to delete it.

Second, if you simply want to delete a program icon or a program group from the Program Manager, you need to use the Delete command within the Program Manager. It does not really erase files from the disk; it simply removes the icon associated with the program or program group from the desktop.

Pertinent Commands

Change Attributes, File Manager
Confirmation Options, File Manager
Delete, File Manager
Delete, Program Manager

Related Tasks

Deleting a Program
Selecting Multiple Files

DELETING A PRINT JOB

I have been sending files to a nonexistent printer for
a few hours without realizing it. I think they may
still be in the Print Manager waiting to print. How
do I check this, and then delete them?

Notes

The Print Manager is a spooling program; it is a
utility that helps you manage what you want to
print. When you open the Print Manager icon, you
will be shown a list of jobs waiting to print. Each of
these jobs is either saved in your computer's
memory or on your computer's disk.

If you want to delete one of the jobs you see listed,
select the job and click on the Delete button. If you
are not using a mouse, select the job and press
ALT-D. The job will be deleted and not printed.

You should also make sure that the Alert Status,
accessed through the Print Manager, is set to a

choice that will alert you when errors exist (like nonexistent or nonresponsive printers).

Pertinent Commands

Alert Always, Print Manager
Flash if Inactive, Print Manager
Ignore if Inactive, Print Manager

Related Tasks

Pausing a Print Job
Resuming a Print Job

DELETING A PROGRAM

How do I delete a program that appears on my desktop?

Notes

This is a two-step process. First, you must delete the program (or program group) using the Delete command within the Program Manager. This command does not really remove the program files from the disk, however. It simply removes the icon associated with the program or program group from the desktop.

After you have deleted the icon, open the File Manager and use the Delete command to delete the actual program files. Make sure that you know which files to delete. There is no clear-cut guideline for this; you just have to do some research to discover which files are used by the program you want to delete.

The Delete command allows you to delete one or more files, or an entire subdirectory. All you need to do is select the files or directories you wish to delete, and then either invoke the Delete command or press the Del key.

Pertinent Commands

Delete, File Manager
Delete, Program Manager

Related Tasks

Deleting a File

DETERMINING THE OPERATING MODE

How do I determine what operating mode Windows is using on my computer?

Notes

If you start Windows simply by typing **WIN** at the DOS prompt, or if Windows starts automatically when you boot your computer, you may find it interesting to know which operating mode it started in. Windows can use any of three operational modes: real mode, standard mode, or 386 enhanced mode.

To determine the operating mode Windows is using, go to the Program Manager. Pull down the Help menu, and select About Program Manager... The window that is displayed will indicate the operating mode.

If you want more information about Windows'
operating modes, refer to the first section of this
pocket reference.

Related Tasks

Using Older Software

ENDING WINDOWS

How do I get out of Windows?

Notes

There are four ways to end your Windows session:

1.   Double-click on the Control Menu icon for the
     Program Manager window.

2.   With the Program Manager active, use the
     Close Window command (accessed by
     pressing ALT-F4).

3.   Use the Exit Windows command from the
     Program Manager.

4.   From the Task List (accessed with the Switch
     To command) choose the Program Manager
     and click on the End Task button.

Before you end Windows, make sure all your
applications have been ended and the appropriate
data files are closed.

It is a good idea to never end Windows by simply
turning off your computer. This can lead to later
problems with your programs if they are processing
data when the computer is turned off.

Pertinent Commands

Close Window, System-wide
Exit Windows, Program Manager
Switch To, System-wide

Related Tasks

Starting Windows

FORMATTING A DISK

How do I format a disk?

Notes

If you want to format a floppy diskette, use the Format Diskette command from within the File Manager. This will allow you to format a floppy diskette in any drive that uses the floppy drive icon, shown here:

If you want the diskette to be bootable, once you choose the Format Diskette command, choose the Make System Disk option.

If you want to format a hard drive, you will have to do so from the DOS prompt. Windows does not allow you to format hard drives.

Pertinent Commands

Format Diskette, File Manager

Suggestions

Make sure the disk you want to format is blank.
Format Diskette is a destructive command; it will
erase any data on the floppy disk being formatted.

GETTING HELP

When I'm working with Windows, I often need a
little help. Is there a fast way I can get it?

Notes

Help is only a keypress away (or so the saying
goes). Windows 3 has a full-featured Help System
that you can even expand with your own input. You
can access the Help System at any time by simply
using the pull-down Help menu, or by pressing `F1`

Pertinent Commands

Annotate, Help System
Copy, Help System
Define Bookmark, Help System
Open File, Help System
Print Topic, Help System
Printer Setup, Help System

Suggestions

If you find yourself referring to the same help
sections again and again, you may want to define a
few bookmarks using the Define Bookmark
command to make finding that troublesome
command easier.

MAKING A SYSTEM DISK

I need a floppy disk that I can use to boot another system. Is there anything special I have to do, other than to format the disk?

Notes

Formatting a diskette only prepares it to hold information. It organizes the disk and sets up the structure used by DOS and Windows. If you want to make a diskette bootable, you need to create a system disk. This is a disk that has special system files on it. These files contain DOS and enable a computer to complete the booting process.

There are two ways to make a system disk. The first is to place the special system files on the disk as it is formatted. This is done if you select the Make System Disk option when you use the Format Diskette command. The other method uses the Make System Diskette command, and assumes you have previously formatted the diskette. Refer to the appropriate sections of the Command Reference for more information on these commands.

Pertinent Commands

Format Diskette, File Manager
Make System Diskette, File Manager

Related Tasks

Formatting a Disk

MAXIMIZING WINDOWS

I am having a hard time reading the application
window I am using. How do I make it larger?

Notes

There are two ways to make windows larger. The
first is to change the window size, which is done by
adjusting the window borders. For more
information on this, see the task Changing the
Window Size.

The other method is to *maximize* the window. This
makes it as large as possible, usually covering the
entire screen. This is done in one of two ways:

- If you are using a mouse, click on the
  maximize button. This is a button with an
  upward-pointing arrow, located in the upper-
  right corner of the window.

- If you are not using a mouse, use the
  Maximize Window command.

Either method will maximize the window, and
should cure any problems brought about by having
a workspace that is too small.

Pertinent Commands

Maximize Window, System-wide

Related Tasks

Changing Window Sizes
Minimizing Windows

MINIMIZING WINDOWS

My desktop is getting cluttered. How do I shrink some windows so they are as small as possible?

Notes

There are two ways to make windows smaller. The first is to change the window size, which is done by moving the window borders. For more information on this, see the task Changing Window Sizes.

The other method (and the one more appropriate to the question) is to *minimize* the window. This makes it as small as possible, shrinking the window to a single icon. This is done in one of two ways:

- If you are using a mouse, click on the minimize button. This is a button with an upward-pointing arrow, located in the upper-right corner of the window.

- If you are not using a mouse, use the Minimize Window command.

Pertinent Commands

Minimize on Use, Program Manager *or* File Manager
Minimize Window, System-wide

Suggestions

You can use the Minimize on Use command within the Program Manager or File Manager to cause these programs to minimize automatically when you run an application from them.

MOVING A FILE

How do I move a file from one directory to another?

Notes

Moving files is similar to copying them. In fact, moving is nothing more than copying and then deleting the original. You move files from within the File Manager.

Once in the File Manager, select the file or files you wish to move. Then, use the Move File command to specify where you want to move them. If you are using a mouse, open both the source and destination directories as individual windows. Then you can drag the files to be moved to their new location.

If you are not using a mouse, you must use the Move File command and enter the complete path for the destination of the files to be moved. While this may sound more difficult, it is pretty easy as long as you have a firm handle on where the files should end up.

Pertinent Commands

Copy File, File Manager
Move, Program Manager
Move File, File Manager

Related Tasks

Copying a File
Formatting a Disk

Moving a Program
Selecting Multiple Files

Suggestions

If you are moving files to a floppy diskette, make
sure it is formatted first. You cannot store
information on an unformatted diskette.

MOVING A PROGRAM

How do I move a program from one window of the
Program Manager to another?

Notes

Moving a program is similar to moving a file, except
all operations occur in the Program Manager.

First, you need to select the program icon you wish
to move. If you are using a mouse, open the source
program group. Then drag the icon to its new
location. This location can be either another open
program group window, or a program group icon.

If you are not using a mouse, you must use the
Move command and enter the name of the program
group to which the program should be moved. If
you can't remember the names of all the program
groups, you can browse through them by clicking on
the arrow at the right of the default group.

Pertinent Commands

Move, Program Manager

Related Tasks

Copying a Program
Moving a File

PAUSING A PRINT JOB

I am using the Print Manager, but want to pause the
file I have just printed so that I can make some
printer adjustments. How do I do this?

Notes

The Print Manager is a spooling program; it is a
utility that helps you manage what you want to
print. When you open the Print Manager icon, you
will be shown a list of jobs waiting to print, as well
as printers that the Print Manager recognizes.

If you want to pause what is going to one of the
printers, select the printer and click on the Pause
button. If you are not using a mouse, select the
printer and press ALT-P. A small icon will appear to
the left of the printer line, and nothing will be sent
to the printer until you choose to resume printing.

Related Tasks

Deleting a Print Job
Resuming a Print Job

PRINTING

OK, I give up! How do I print?

Notes

For some strange reason, in Windows you can usually find the printer-related commands listed under the File menu. Before you can choose the Print command (this sends the actual output to your printer), there are a few steps you must do:

1. Make sure you have installed the correct printer drivers. See the Adding a Printer task for more information.

2. Make sure you have selected the right hardware port for the printer.

3. Make sure you have configured and set up the printer correctly.

4. Make sure the printer is turned on, on-line, and available for use.

5. If you are using the Print Manager, make sure that output to the printer is not paused.

6. Make sure your information is formatted in the desired fashion. (This is entirely dependant on the application program you are using.)

If you do all these things, you should be able to get your output using the Print command.

Pertinent Commands

Alert Always, Print Manager
Change System Settings, Setup
Flash if Inactive, Print Manager
High Priority, Print Manager
Ignore if Inactive, Print Manager
Low Priority, Print Manager
Medium Priority, Print Manager

Print File, File Manager
Print Topic, Help System
Printer Settings, Control Panel
Printer Setup, Help System

Related Tasks

Adding a Printer
Changing Printers
Changing the Default Printer
Pausing a Print Job
Resuming a Print Job
Setting Paper Orientation

Suggestions

The first time you use Windows with a printer, or
the first time you use a new printer with Windows,
make sure you are not rushed. Give yourself plenty
of time to get used to the new system and
comfortable with its capabilities.

REMOVING A PRINTER

I have upgraded my printer, and I successfully
added the new printer driver to Windows. How do I
delete the old printer driver, since I don't need it
any more?

Notes

Removing a printer driver is a much easier process
than adding a printer. To remove a printer, open

the Printers icon from the Control Panel. From the list of printer drivers in the upper-left corner of the dialog box, select the printer to be removed. Click on the Configure button, and then on Remove. Windows will ask you to confirm your action; if you do so, the printer driver is removed from the list of available printers.

The printer drivers you have removed will not really be removed until you click the OK button on the Printers dialog box. If you click on Cancel, or press Esc, the removal is not completed.

If you later decide you wish to add the printer driver, you will have to go through the process of adding a printer again.

Pertinent Commands

Printer Settings, Control Panel

Related Tasks

Changing Printers
Changing the Default Printer

Suggestions

Keeping the old printer driver installed does not hurt anything. You may want to simply configure it so that it is not active or so that output for that printer goes to a file. That way, if you ever get visiting rights for your old printer, you will still be able to print a file through it.

RENAMING A FILE

How do I change the name of a file?

Notes

If you want to change the name of a program file in the Program Manager, see the task Renaming a Program.

You can change filenames using the File Manager. This is done with the Rename command. Actually, you can use this command to rename directories or files. There are only a few conditions under which you cannot do a rename:

- You cannot rename the root directory of a drive.

- You cannot rename a file that has the read-only file attribute enabled.

- You cannot rename a file or directory to a name already in use by another file in the same directory.

When you use the Rename command, you are shown the old name of the file or directory, and asked to enter a new name. Names should follow the same rules as names for files; they should be eight characters or less with up to three characters for an extension. The extension should be separated from the rest of the filename by a period. You cannot enter a disk drive designation in the new name. If you do, you will get an error message.

Pertinent Commands

Rename, File Manager

Related Tasks

Copying a File
Creating a Directory
Deleting a File
Moving a File
Renaming a Program

Suggestions

Be careful in renaming files and directories. If you
rename program files that are used elsewhere in
Windows, then Windows will not be able to find the
program unless you make additional changes. If
you change the name of data files needed by
application programs, it is possible those programs
will not be able to function properly because
Windows is not able to find the data files.

RENAMING A PROGRAM

How do I rename a program shown in the Program
Manager?

Notes

Renaming programs in the Program Manager is
really quite simple. The name shown under the
program icon and at the top of the application
window is completely under your control.

To change the program name, select the program icon whose name you wish to change. Then use the Properties command and change the description line. That's it.

Pertinent Commands

Properties, Program Manager

Related Tasks

Adding Applications
Deleting a Program
Renaming a File

Suggestions

Windows comes with program names that are good for general purposes, but if you would rather see different names, then change them. This will have no affect on anything else you do in Windows.

RESUMING A PRINT JOB

I am using the Print Manager, and I previously paused output to a printer. How do I resume printing my files?

Notes

The Print Manager is a spooling program; it is a utility that helps you manage what you want to print. When you open the Print Manager icon, you will be shown a list of jobs waiting to print, as well as printers that the Print Manager recognizes. If a printer has been paused, a small icon will appear to the left of the printer line.

To resume printing to a printer, select one that has been paused (it has the icon), and click on the Resume button. If you are not using a mouse, select the printer and press Alt-R. Information should start flowing to the printer right away.

Related Tasks

Deleting a Print Job
Pausing a Print Job

RUNNING A PROGRAM

How do I run a program from Windows?

Notes

There are several ways to run programs within Windows:

- Use the Run command from either the Program Manager or File Manager. When you choose this, you must provide the program name and any parameters necessary to run the program.

- Select the icon for the program you want to run, and then issue the Open command.

- If you are using a mouse, double-click on the icon for the program you want to run. This can be either a program item icon (in the Program Manager) or an icon for an EXE, COM, BAT, or PIF file in the File Manager.

- In the File Manager, select a file that has been attached to a program. Open the file.

- If you are using a mouse and are in the File Manager, drag the icon for a data file onto the top of the program icon.

Regardless of the method used, the effect is still the same. Windows attempts to load the file and execute the program.

If you attempt to open a non-Windows program, it is possible that it will not run in the Windows environment. If you find this is the case, you may be able to solve the problem through the use of PIF files for the application. Creating, maintaining, and using PIF files is beyond the scope of this pocket reference. For more information, refer to *Windows 3: The Complete Reference* by Tom Sheldon.

Pertinent Commands

Open, Program Manager *or* File Manager
Run, Program Manager *or* File Manager

Related Tasks

Stopping a Program
Using Older Software

SEARCHING FOR FILES

I have so many files on my hard drive, I find it virtually impossible to remember where they all are. How do I find files on my hard drive?

Notes

You can search for files from within the File
Manager. Use the Search for Files command to look
for files either in the current directory or across the
entire disk.

Before you use the Search for Files command, make
sure you have selected the disk drive you wish to
search. After you select the command, you are
prompted for the file specification to use when
searching. You can specify partial names or get
really fancy with this parameter. Full discussion of
filenames and wildcard characters is beyond the
scope of this pocket reference. For more
information, see *Simply DOS* or *DOS: The Complete
Reference, Third Edition*, both by Kris Jamsa.

If you want to search the entire disk, select the
Search Entire Disk option. When you press Enter or
click on the OK button, the File Manager will
compile a list of files that match your specification.
These are presented in the Search Results window.

Pertinent Commands

Search for Files, File Manager

Related Tasks

Selecting Multiple Files

SELECTING MULTIPLE FILES

I need to delete a group of files. How do I select a
group of files?

Notes

Typically, the File Manager only acts on the highlighted file. You can select multiple files, which is referred to as building a selection set, in any of several ways.

- If you are entering a filename when prompted by a command, you can use DOS wildcard characters. Full discussion of wildcard characters is beyond the scope of this pocket reference. For more information, see *Simply DOS* or *DOS: The Complete Reference, Third Edition*, both by Kris Jamsa and published by Osborne/McGraw-Hill.

- If you are using a mouse, you can click on the first filename you want in the selection set. Then, while holding down the SHIFT key, click on the last filename for the selection set. All files between the first and last filenames will be highlighted.

- If you are using a mouse, you can hold down the CTRL key and click on the files you want in the selection set. Each file you click on is highlighted and added to the selection set.

- Use the Select All command to select all files in the current window.

- Use the Search for Files command to create a window that lists files based on your specific search criteria. Then you can use any method previously listed to build your selection set.

Pertinent Commands

Select All, File Manager
Search for Files, File Manger

Related Tasks

Searching for Files

SELECTING WINDOWS

How do I choose the active window?

Notes

If you are using a mouse, you can choose the active window simply by clicking on the left mouse button anywhere within a window.

If you are not using a mouse, the process is a little more complex. You can use any of the following control keys:

CTRL-F6   Selects the next document window or icon in the current application window.

CTRL-TAB   Same as CTRL-F6 ; selects the next document window or icon in the current application window.

CTRL-SHIFT-TAB   This does the reverse of CTRL-TAB ; cycles through the document windows and icons in reverse order in the current applications window.

CTRL-ESC   Displays the Task List window, from which you can select among the currently open application windows.

ALT-ESC   Selects the next application window.

If you are working solely with document windows, you can also use the Next Window command from the Control menu. This will cause the next document window to become active.

Pertinent Commands

Next Window, System-wide

Related Tasks

Changing Window Sizes
Maximizing Windows
Minimizing Windows

SETTING PAPER ORIENTATION

I have one of these fancy laser printers. How do I make my file print sideways on the paper?

Notes

There are two ways to orient text and graphics on a piece of paper. These are called *portrait orientation* and *landscape orientation*. The following illustrates the difference between the two:

Portrait orientation has the text or pictures running parallel to the short side of the paper just like a portrait in an art gallery; landscape has them running parallel to the long side.

For laser printers you can change the orientation of your paper through the Printer Settings command. Open the Printers icon within the Control Panel. Then, from the list in the upper-left corner of the dialog box, select the printer you are going to use. Now click on the Configure button, and then on the Setup button.

If Windows is capable of controlling the paper orientation of your printer, you will see a place to set this in the lower-left corner of the dialog box. Select whether you want portrait or landscape orientation. Click on the OK button three times, and you are ready to begin printing.

It is also possible that some application programs allow you to change paper orientation. For instance, you can change orientation from the Write accessory, or with the Printer Setup command of the Help System.

Pertinent Commands

Printer Settings, Control Panel
Printer Setup, Help System

Related Tasks

Adding a Printer
Changing Printers
Changing the Default Printer

Suggestions

If you print a variety of documents with your
printer, don't forget to change the paper orientation
before each printing.

> ## SETTING THE DATE AND TIME

Daylight savings time has just kicked in, and I need
to change the time on my computer. How do I do
this?

Notes

Internally, your computer system keeps track of the
time and date. Windows accesses this information
in order to control some functions. For instance, the
Appointment accessory uses the date and time
information to operate properly.

Changing the date and time is a simple task. All
you need to do is open the Date/Time icon on the
Control Panel. You will see a display of both the
date and time, which you can modify either by
typing in new information, or by using the up and
down control buttons to change it.

If you want to change the format in which the date
and time are displayed, you can use the
International Settings command.

Pertinent Commands

Date & Time Settings, Control Panel
International Settings, Control Panel

Suggestions

If you only have to change the time by a single hour, highlight the hour in the Time box, and click on the upward- or downward-pointing arrow. This causes the time to increase or decrease by exactly one hour.

STARTING WINDOWS

What are all the ways in which I can start Windows?

Notes

There are several ways to start Windows. The usual way is simply to type **WIN** and press Enter at the DOS prompt. However, you can include some command-line parameters that will modify the way Windows starts up. These parameters are

/R   Start Windows in real mode. You might want to do this if you have a specific Windows application that is not written to work with Windows 3.

/S   Start Windows in standard mode. This is an "in-between" mode that is more powerful than real mode, but not as powerful as 386 enhanced mode. You would use this mode if you have a 386 computer and are limited on memory, or if you cannot get Windows to function properly on your computer in 386 enhanced mode.

/3   Start Windows in 386 enhanced mode. To do this you must have a 386- or 486-based computer with at least 2MB of memory. In this mode, Windows 3 takes full advantage of your hardware and offers the best operating platform.

You can use any of these switches to change the operating mode, but you cannot use more than one at a time.

In addition to the mode switch, you can also specify a command line (after the mode switch) that you want Windows to run after starting. This is the same type of command line you would enter if you were using the Run command.

Pertinent Commands

Run, Program Manager *or* File Manager

Related Tasks

Ending Windows

STOPPING A PROGRAM

How do I stop an application?

Notes

There are several ways to stop an application. These include

- Choose Exit from within the application. This command can usually be found under the File menu.

- If you are using a mouse, double-click on the Control Menu icon.

- Use the Close Window command.
- Use the Switch To command to pull up the Task List. Select the application you want to end, and then select the End Task button.

Any of these choices will effectively do the same thing. Select the method you are most comfortable with.

Pertinent Commands

Close Window, System-wide
Switch To, System-wide

Related Tasks

Running a Program

USING OLDER SOFTWARE

I have some software written for an older version of Windows. I still need to use it, but I can't seem to make it work. How come?

Notes

If at all possible, Windows always begins in its most powerful mode, 386 enhanced mode. Some software written for earlier versions of Windows will not work with this operating mode. When attempting to run the program, Windows will check and make sure the software is compatible with the current operating mode. If it isn't, Windows will display a dialog box informing you of this.

Older software can usually be run if you start Windows in real mode. This is done by following these steps:

1. Exit Windows, returning all the way to the DOS prompt.

2. Change to the subdirectory that contains Windows.

3. From the DOS prompt, issue the command **WIN /R**.

Windows will now load and run in real mode. You should be able to load your old software and use it with no further problems.

If you want more information about Windows' operating modes, refer to the first section of this pocket reference.

Pertinent Commands

Open, Program Manager *or* File Manager
Run, Program Manager *or* File Manager

Related Tasks

Determining the Operating Mode
Ending Windows
Running a Program

USING THE CLIPBOARD

How do I use the Clipboard?

Notes

The Clipboard is an integral part of virtually every application program written for Windows. It is the Clipboard that allows you to Cut, Copy, and Paste.

When you use the Cut or Copy editing commands available on the Edit menu of most application programs, the information you have selected, whether it is text or graphics, is copied into the Clipboard. Whatever was in the Clipboard before is lost; only the most recent Cut or Copy is retained. Later, when you use the Paste command, the information in the Clipboard is inserted at the location of your cursor.

When you quit your application program, the contents of the Clipboard are not disturbed. You can then start another program and paste the old Clipboard information into a document in that program.

Besides using the Clipboard with application software, you can actually open the Clipboard and operate on it directly. The Clipboard is available as a program within the Program Manager.

When you open the Clipboard icon, you are shown what it contains. You can then use a variety of commands (all available from the Clipboard menu) to process the information in the Clipboard.

Pertinent Commands

Delete Clipboard, Clipboard
Open Clipboard File, Clipboard
Save As, Clipboard

USING THE TASK LIST

What is the Task List, and how do I use it?

Notes

The Task List is an internal list, maintained by Windows, of all applications currently running. *Tasks* are individual programs running under Windows. The Task List is the main switching point for applications running at the same time.

To access the Task List, use the Switch To command. This is available from the Control menu in an application window, or you can call it up by pressing Ctrl–Esc. If you are using a mouse, you can double-click anywhere on the desktop (outside of any open window). The following is an example of a Task List:

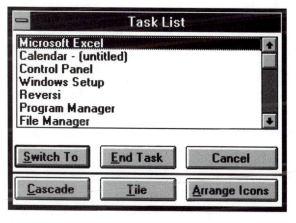

Notice the full list of currently open applications. You can select a task and press Enter, double-click on a task, or click on a task and click on the Switch

To button, and that task will be switched to the foreground. You can also terminate programs using this command by selecting a task and then clicking on the End Task button.

The bottom three buttons on the Task List window are for arranging application windows and icons. You can experiment with them if you want to see what effect they will have on your desktop. They will not affect how the programs run.

Pertinent Commands

Switch To, System-wide

Related Tasks

Running a Program
Stopping a Program

Index